THE CERTAINTY OF ETERNITY

THE CERTAINTY OF ETERNITY

by

L. C. DANBY

www.whitecrowbooks.com

The Certainty of Eternity

Copyright © 2013 by Jo Buchanan. All rights reserved.

Published and printed in the United States of America and the United Kingdom by White Crow Books; an imprint of White Crow Productions Ltd.

No part of this book may be reproduced, copied or used in any form or manner whatsoever without written permission, except in the case of brief quotations in reviews and critical articles.

For information, contact White Crow Books
at 3 Merrow Grange, Guildford, GU1 2QW United Kingdom,
or e-mail to info@whitecrowbooks.com.

Cover Designed by Butterflyeffect
Interior design by Velin@Perseus-Design.com

Paperback ISBN 978-1-910121-34-4
eBook   ISBN 978-1-910121-35-1

Non Fiction / Body, Mind & Spirit / Parapsychology

www.whitecrowbooks.com

Disclaimer: White Crow Productions Ltd. and its directors, employees, distributors, retailers, wholesalers and assignees disclaim any liability or responsibility for the author's statements, words, ideas, criticisms or observations. White Crow Productions Ltd. assumes no responsibility for errors, inaccuracies, or omissions.

To my wife, Anne
whose sensible advice and encouragement
in compiling this book were invaluable

I am fully convinced that the soul is indestructible, and that its activity will continue through Eternity.
>   GOETHE

Death but supplies the oil for the inextinguishable lamp of Life.
>   COLERIDGE

God is not the God of the Dead, but of the Living.
>   JESUS OF NAZARETH

Truth is strange, stranger than fiction.
>   LORD BYRON

Stan, Leslie, Bert

CONTENTS

FOREWORD xi
PREFACE xv
INTRODUCTION xix
1. Who Are the Mediums? 1
2. The Achilles Heel of Spiritualism 5
3. An Uncomplicated Man 9
4. A Gift Accepted 13
5. The University of Experience 17
6. Spiritual Teachers 25
7. The Inner Circle 31
8. Unprogressed Spirits 35
9. A Blueprint for Eternity 41
10. An Awakening 45
11. The Challenge 51
12. They Were All Amazed 55
13. An Angel of Joy 61

14. The Power of Thought 65

15. To Travel Without Body.. 69

16. Apports and Materialized Gifts 77

17. Automatic Painting... 87

18. Direct Voice Communication 95

19. A Thousand Spirit Voices 101

20. Luminosity... 109

21. Inspiration... 123

22. A Prophet of Modern Times 127

23. His Greatest Friend... 135

24. The Teachings of the Guides 141

25. The Purpose of It All... 151

26. His Task Well Done 155

27. A Cross of Light 159

28. An Inspiration to Carry Forward.. 163

29. A Practical Plan.. 167

Eye Witnesses 175

FOREWORD

This book is about Stan Walsh, one of Australia's most respected and talented physical mediums of the early 20th century.

My father L. C. Danby, sat in Walsh's home circle for a number of years, and *The Certainty of Eternity* is his account of those years.

Stan Walsh died in 1939 so the grieving over his death still existed when I was born in 1940.

The most distinguishing feature of spiritualism is the belief that the soul lives on after physical death and can be communicated with. The bulk of my father's activity in spiritualist circles occurred in the years after the death of his first wife, before he met my Mum and became involved in the Presbyterian Church. Despite this, he maintained a passionate interest in spiritualism for the rest of his life.

Dad started up another development circle some years after my sister Christine was born in 1942. The arrival of people to our house on Friday nights for weekly séances was accepted routine for my sister and I, like saying grace at meal times. We were given drawings of our spirit guides and told they were there to protect and guide us, just as guardian angels protected Roman Catholics. My guide was a Native American 'squaw' called White Bird, who had come through regularly in Stan Walsh's group. The Native American leather bonnet that had been materialised had allegedly been worn by her before she passed over. As a child, I loved it and always wore it when we played Cowboys and Indians with the other kids in the street.

Christine and I didn't realise that séances and spirit guides were not a regular part of other peoples' lives. For a while we were protected by our innocence but when I entered my teens in the 1950s, nobody warned me it was best not to talk about the goings-on at our house on Friday nights. When I did, the looks on peoples' faces comprised a mixture of derision, horror and concern for my mental health. I very quickly stopped.

When we were teenagers, Christine and I began conducting our own secret séances. Neither of us appeared to possess the gift of mediumship so we opted for a ouija board made from a large sheet of cardboard. I wrote the alphabet in a circle on the board, each side of the circle separated by the word YES at the top and NO at the bottom. We used a penny for a planchette and began proceedings with the Lord's Prayer, doing it at night when Mum and Dad had retired to the lounge room to read or listen to classical records on the radiogram. If Dad had ever found out, we'd have been in big trouble. He believed ouija boards were portals to un-progressed spirits and all hell could break loose. Sometimes we did it on Saturday afternoons while Mum and Dad worked in the garden.

Sitting cross-legged on the bedroom floor, we'd lean forward solemnly, place our forefingers on the planchette and ask questions.

'Is anyone there?'

If the penny moved to the word YES, we'd enquire piously, 'Do you come in the name of Jesus Christ?'

If it answered YES, we would continue.

'Will Eric ask me out?'

'What am I meant to do in life?'

'Is there a separate heaven for animals?'

We tried to solve murder mysteries we heard about on the wireless.

'Is that Max Stuart guilty of the murder in Western Australia?'

'If not, who is?'

Sometimes the penny would race across the board so quickly that we couldn't keep up and the coin shot off the surface. On these occasions it was obvious to us that powerful invisible entities were at work. At other times, the penny appeared devoid of animation and didn't budge, prompting us to pack up and try again another day. We never consciously cheated by pushing the penny. Whether we did so subconsciously, I will never know.

It was around this time that Dad started writing *The Certainty of Eternity*. Years later, when the book was published and Dad had to do publicity for it, he was interviewed by journalist and radio presenter

Claudia Wright on radio station 3AW. Just as she was asking him questions about the existence of 'spirits' the electricity in the radio station suddenly and unaccountably switched itself off and then on again. Much ado was made of the incident, Claudia Wright milking it for all it was worth, and the Melbourne *Sun* newspaper devoted a whole page to the contents of Dad's book.

Spiritualism is often ridiculed, due to charlatans and those motivated by self-aggrandising who give it a bad name. The members of Stan Walsh's group were people whose sole concern were to become educated in higher principles. Money was never exchanged at any time.

I am grateful for my parents' legacy of faith. I don't like some of the human input to religion. Most religious people live by their teachings but there are always some who are judgemental of another's religion, or misinterpret ancient words or behave in a hypocritical manner.

I like the concepts of spiritualism. I also like the Buddha's teachings. I especially like the spiritual teachings of the Native American who treat the forests, waterways and the air we breathe with the same reverence as they treat the life force of humans and animals. They believe all things are connected like the threads of a giant web and if we damage one thread of the web, it automatically affects the whole.

My parents still visit me in my dreams sometimes. When I wake up, it is often with the perfect answer to a problem; or just a warm, comforting feeling that I am not alone.

Jo Buchanan,
Australia, 2013

PREFACE

A book called *Honest To God* by John A. T. Robinson, Bishop of Woolwich, was published in England by the S.C.M. Press in 1963. It created an ecclesiastical uproar. Criticism of it—for and against—was collected by David L. Edwards and compiled into a book, also published by the S.C.M. Press in England, titled, *The Honest To God Debate*. In this the editor said: The clergy agree that the questions the Bishop of Woolwich pose are real and important, but many doubt whether the questions are adequate'. Edwards went on to state: 'Questions asked by people in the church, on the fringe, and beyond it, are NOT answered—questions such as:

> What is the purpose of life?
> What is wrong with me?
> What lies beyond death?'

The purpose of this book, is to endeavour to answer these questions. By sharing with others my knowledge and experiences of a man whom I considered one of the world's greatest mediums and, indeed, a prophet of modem times, the answers naturally unfold. The man whose life and spiritual work is explained through this book was named Stan Walsh. He was an ordinary carpenter whose cross, and privilege, it was to bear the responsibility of having extraordinary mystical powers; powers never sought by himself, but accepted humbly as the will of God.

The remarkable gifts showered upon him from Divine Sources, and the amazing and constant flow of proofs of the continuation of life after death which were revealed through him, are explained as faithfully as the author knows how in these pages.

In compiling this work it has been seen as important to point out experiences which show beyond doubt that many of the incidents recorded in the Bible, especially the New Testament, were indeed true events and how so many of the teachings and prophecies made then are still valid today.

Further, I hope that these revelations will bring comfort and understanding and give new faith, and zest for living not only to bereaved readers, but to all deep thinking people who, in spite of their beliefs, find it more and more difficult to see any real meaning or purpose to life. They prove, in many ways, that there is a Divine Force which is NOT dead, in spite of declarations to the contrary, and that the Universe is pervaded by the omnipotent all-loving spirit of God.

There is a striking message in this book for the younger generation. Although Stan Walsh lived and worked out his life for his people long before most of today's spiritually sensitive young people were born, he was very much tuned in to the higher vibrations now being felt by so many in the raised consciousness of the present age.

Walsh gave himself to be an instrument for the bringing down of special knowledge and messages of peace from higher planes to a world about to be plunged into its darkest period in all history. As early as 1930 the Second World War was prophesied through him. It was predicted as a war that would be 'the ghastliest ever known by man'.

We have emerged from this dark time and today's generation has been born into a much brighter world—but there are still shadows, fears and uncertainties. It is therefore important to understand that the messages of solace and hope which were held as beacons of light for so many a generation ago, are still valid. There is no turning off the kind of light brought down by an instrument such as Walsh.

Much of the special wisdom brought to the world through Stan Walsh's mediumship in the 1930s can be understood even more clearly today. The peace and enlightenment that he was instrumental in bringing to so many souls during his own lifetime can be tapped again in this day just as effectively. For those who still need reassurance in this spiritually enlivened age, his oft-repeated reassurances leave no doubt of the certainty of Eternity and the everlasting destiny of the human soul.

Walsh's spiritual mission on earth lasted until his body died in 1939. His ministry profoundly affected the lives of many people from every walk of life and from almost every creed, belief and denomination. It also brought about a spiritual awakening in the souls of many who had called themselves agnostics or atheists. The author is one of these.

In spite of all this, Stan Walsh was never a public figure. His meetings were held in private homes, not his own, and those who attended came always by invitation. The church proper barely heard of him, and when it did, remained unconcerned.

Walsh was supported in his early years by an earnest band of five people known as the Inner Circle. They met three times a week in various Melbourne suburbs. Later, when high spiritual developments took place, outsiders were invited to witness the extraordinary spiritual phenomena revealed and hear inspiring lectures by high spiritual personalities, many of them Biblical entities who controlled Walsh's body and mind. Others were invited to be given the opportunity to communicate, through Walsh, with so-called dead relatives and friends and to be thus convinced, beyond all doubt, of the immortality of the soul—the certainty of Eternity.

L. C. Danby

INTRODUCTION

This is the story of the extraordinary mediumistic gifts given to an ordinary working man.

Mediums are unique to us only in that they can make contact with invisible intelligences and manifest spiritual powers not their own. All human beings have mediumistic abilities to some extent. An isolated flash from the unknown may be unexpectedly revealed to their astonished minds, often when they least expect it; a still, small voice may suddenly speak within them, or a strong, overpowering thought invade their conscious mind, that may move them to do or to act in a forthright manner that is regarded by their relatives or friends as eminently wise, sensible or prudent. The recipient may merely call it a 'hunch'—a colloquial term for a flash of 'inspiration'. Fully developed mediums are simply more developed in this respect.

Actually the highest form of mediumship is that which is practised by many spiritual people who make it their habit to retire for a short time each day into a quiet corner, to silently pray to God for guidance. Their mental prayer is couched in simple words in which they give thanks to God for all blessings received, and then they ask Him simply for advice or help in solving some problem or receiving some instruction as to how they can help someone who is in distress. They then try and 'still' their minds for a few minutes, hoping to receive a Divine Thought that will help them in this direction. People who practise this form of spiritual communication with God have learnt to be sincere and honest, and have the faith of a child.

Stan Walsh, the medium of this story, was, in his later years, in the habit of practising this private form of mediumship and it was one of the reasons for the continued development of his gifts. His gifts were many and eventually developed to a stage regarded by some as miraculous. They were certainly beyond ordinary human understanding and they included clairvoyance, clairaudience and an astonishing degree of mediumship.

Walsh's public mediumship was conducted under deep trance; that is, he would allow his body to be temporarily taken possession of by his special spiritual guides from the spirit world, or by other spirit entities allowed by these guides, while he himself surrendered to a state of trance or temporary non-possession of his body.

When referring to the words: 'Deep Trance' or to 'Spirits' in this book I am merely adopting words used in the Bible, and with the same meaning. Balaam, for instance, was described as being 'in a trance' when he prophesied about Israel in Numbers: Chapter 24:Verse 2. Again, 'trance' is mentioned in the New Testament many times. In Acts: Chapter 10: Verse 10, Peter is described as 'being in a trance' and is so described again in Chapter 11: Verse 17.

There are countless incidents in the Bible where it is recorded that the Prophets 'heard voices' (a gift nowadays called clairaudience) or 'saw visions' (a gift nowadays known as clairvoyance) or were 'tranced'. There are also many reports of 'spirit possession' or 'demon possession' which is the same thing. 'Demons' or, more correctly 'unprogressed spirits' can, and still do, obsess many people these days especially those who mindlessly dabble in frivolous spiritualistic séances or table-rapping sessions, etc.

Unless understood, and handled with due reverence and earnestness, this careless calling upon the spirits of the dead can be a dangerous pastime.

Many of Walsh's gifts bear striking likeness to those recorded in scripture and in descriptions found elsewhere in history. One of these gifts was the gift of luminosity. It was a remarkable gift, but Stan Walsh was by no means the first human luminary and the purpose in such a gift is well understood by Christians who believe that the light of God is the 'hidden force' behind the whole structure of their religion. Jesus, the 'Light of the World', was by far the greatest human luminary.

His apostle, John, in his first Epistle, Chapter 1, declares that God is not only Love, but also Light. A spark of that Light is carried by every human being in his soul and in those who live worthy lives—lives spent in love of fellow human beings and all creation—this Light shines through to bless, inspire and uplift all who come in contact with It. Jesus, Himself, is the authority for this statement. He said: 'Let your Light so shine before men that they, seeing your good works, shall glorify your Father in Heaven'.

The materialization of Light shown through Walsh by the High Guides was a revelation to the many followers who regularly attended his meetings and to others who came to witness these things. It was not until after his death, however, when they had fully recovered from the shock and the feeling that this Light had 'gone out' with his departure from among them, that Walsh's loyal followers began to realize that although the Light could no longer be seen in the old way, it was to continue to shine, 'unseen' from themselves and from the souls of all who love their fellow men.

As Stan Walsh's mission began in 1919 and it was not until 1927 that I first met him, I have had to obtain the facts relating to those years from eye witnesses whose characters were beyond reproach. From the time when I first met Walsh—the year 1927—I have written the story from my own observations, using my personal records and occasionally collaborating with the statements of others.

It would be logical for the reader of this book to question why the record of Walsh's life has not been made available to the public until now. The author can only answer this by expressing his own feeling that there is a right time for every event in the overall scheme of things, and that NOW is the right time to bring forward, and make more widely public, the knowledge that was brought down by the mediumship of Stan Walsh a generation ago.

The author believes that Walsh's extraordinary experiences were primarily timed to meet the needs of people facing an extraordinary period in history. It could be said that he was 'ahead of his time', but, as we now know, there was good reason for this.

Today there is a readiness for spiritual knowledge that was not so evident in society at the time the revelations were made. Overall, people in the 1970s are more interested in spiritual experiences than in any other decade of this century. Furthermore, there is, today, much evidence of a remarkable leavening in the hearts of men whereby they are now more tolerant to one another's personal beliefs than ever before in recorded history.

Whatever inspiration compels the publishing of Walsh's life story at this time, the fact remains that he was spiritually 'a man for all seasons'. The Light that he was instrumental in bringing down to the darkened world of his day is capable of being turned on again, with whatever measure of brilliance needed, to further guide the way of mankind. At the end of this book I have endeavoured to explain how the Light can again be turned on by any man or woman with a simple faith in God and perfect submission to His Will.

As a matter of interest, there are records of an occasion in 1934 when Hetty, a special and very high spirit guide who was 'assigned' to Walsh to govern the timbre of his meetings, came through and spoke to a Mrs McIntosh, a regular follower, and announced that someday a book, recording the events taking place, would be written and published. At that time the author of this book felt in no way inspired to take up this task nor even suspected that he would ever write such a work. Even now, he does not see this prophecy as being the real motivation for his present effort. The urge to now bring this record before the public would, he feels, have been just as strong had this prophecy not been included in the records.

However, it is an interesting fact and it does exemplify the numerous small prophecies made through Walsh's mediumship, that have come true. Some of these are recorded here, many are not because they related to personal lives at the time, and in any case space would not permit the inclusion of them all.

There are several important prophecies made through Walsh, yet to be fulfilled. To bring these to the notice of the people in this age would be sufficient reason, of itself, to give this book existence at this time. It is, however, to make widely known the life of a man whom the author feels is truly a saint of our own times, and to allow his inspiration and Light to reach further out in the dawning of what is undoubtedly a new age in the history of man, that *The Certainty Of Eternity* has been written.

To give absolute credibility to Stan Walsh's amazing story, I have included reproductions of signed statements from some of his close followers.

In most cases actual names have been used throughout this story, and with full permission of the people concerned or their relatives; in one or two cases real names have been changed for personal reasons. Walsh's many followers are now scattered all over the world. A number still live in Melbourne, Australia, where he practised his mediumship, and, of course, others have now passed on.

In conclusion, while the author vouches for the truth of everything contained in these pages, he warns that truth can be found by those who sincerely search for it. A spiritual truth can always be held up to the light and it is for every intelligent being on every plane of existence to make his own free-willed judgement from the facts made available to him. The most valuable aid to the reception of knowledge is an open mind. Only those who approach new concepts with an open mind can take in knowledge hitherto unknown.

1

WHO ARE THE MEDIUMS?

Seek ye first the Kingdom of God

JESUS OF NAZARETH

Confucius is credited with having said: 'Bemoan not the departed with excessive grief. The dead are devoted and faithful friends; they are ever associated with us.' For centuries men have devoted themselves to the task of trying to learn whether or not this is true. Some have found the search futile; many more have allowed it to lead them over a long trail of spiritual experience. For modern man this can include agnosticism and any or all of the eleven religions of present times.

Invariably, the searcher discovers in some form or other the modern science loosely described as 'psychical research.' This is an area which offers endless possibilities for proving scientifically that man survives after death, and that there is a realistic plan for the Universe and its inhabitants.

Most approach the field of psychic research warily, and wisely so. At the same time the wise seeker after truth realises that he or she must approach this subject with an unbiased, open mind, a mind powered with a genuine wish not only to find truth, but to become an instrument for the sources of truth.

There are many types of human beings, men and women, who are seeking to become special instruments for these sources. They are called 'Mediums', and they are often referred to by others as being 'mediumistic'.

This leads us on to a question which is frequently asked: What is a medium? A common definition of the term 'medium' is: 'A person through whom spirits are said to make themselves seen or heard, or one who, though the agency of spirit forces, can move objects at a distance.'

To a certain extent we are all mediums. Certainly all men and women have the potential for the development of some mediumistic qualities. On the plane in which he exists on earth man is constantly engaged, consciously or unconsciously, in a form of mediumship as he brings into fruition the plans of nature or creation.

It is, however, to that particular and often intriguing form of mediumship that is found in an area commonly called 'the world of spiritualism' to which we turn our attention. Ideally it should be regarded always as a privileged, sacred and absolutely non-exploitable form of mediumship. Unfortunately, as with so many other sacred things in life, this is not always so. In the case of the subject of this book there is no doubt whatsoever that his mediumship was always held, by himself and his followers, with the highest respect.

There are several types of mediums referred to in the world of spiritualism. In spiritualistic terminology they are:

Inspirational mediums: People who are clairvoyant, that is, they can see spirits or spiritual symbols shown to them from the spirit world and people who are clairaudient, that is, those who can hear spirits speak to them or hear voices conveyed to them by spirit forces.

With these two gifts inspirational mediums can give convincing proof to hearers that there is life after death.

Trance mediums: People who are temporarily completely controlled by spirits from the spirit world, that is spirits can dominate every function—mental and physical, including the conscious mind—of the human instrument, or medium. Whilst under this control the medium has no knowledge whatsoever of what the controlling spirit is saying to his or her hearers. The subject of this book was highly endowed with an extremely powerful gift of deep-trance mediumship.

Semi-trance mediums: People who are only partially controlled, that is the spirit speaking through them can only control the speaking apparatus of the medium—it does not control the conscious mind or other functions of the body, as when under complete trance. The result is that the medium is aware of what the spirit is saying to his or her hearers.

Physical-phenomena mediums: People who can move objects from a distance. Among these are those sometimes called 'Trumpet Mediums'. In this case a certain visible force called ectoplasm, issues from the body of the medium which enables spirits to use this ectoplasm to materialise their spirit hands and carry a speaking trumpet around the room. This same ectoplasm also is used by the spirits to materialise their voice-boxes and speak aloud through this trumpet, which amplifies their soft spirit voices, so that hearers can hear what they (the spirits) are saying. Here again, the subject of this book was a Trumpet medium.

Another definition of a trance medium is: 'a person in whose body the etheric matter easily separates from the denser matter'. This separation allows them to become a 'telephone' between the visible and the invisible planes. If the etheric matter of the body is easily extruded, the physical body falls naturally into a trance state, and the mechanism of human vocalization can be operated by the spirit entity who has temporarily taken possession of the medium's body.

Genuine mediums are always protected by high spiritual guides or doorkeepers. This can only be fully explained with detailed examples and, in the course of this book, a clearer understanding of this important aspect of trance mediumship is brought out.

A fundamental necessity, however, for anyone seeking to develop mediumistic power, whether it be Inspirational, Deep-trance or Semi-trance is that their lives must be above reproach. They must seek to become honest, both with themselves and others. Most importantly, they must seek to acquire a simple, child-like faith in God. They should 'seek first the Kingdom of God'; that is, seek to know God's will as to what they should do to develop psychically, and ask for His strength to be given to their guides and loved ones, to make themselves known to him or her, so that they can pass on the knowledge they receive, to their followers or adherents. If they do this it is quite possible that they will find that 'all these things will be added unto them'.

Past history, secular and spiritual, is littered with the names of famous people who were actually 'mediums', although not known as such. Among them were people like St. Benedict, St. Bernard, St. Teresa of Avila and St. Teresa of Lesieux, St. Anthony of the Desert, Monsieur Vianny, the Cure of D'Ars in France, Florence Nightingale, Elizabeth Fry, William Penn, Australia's John Flynn of the Inland, Joan of Arc, and the famous Australian singer, Madame Melba. They were all confronted with definite psychic experiences at some time in their lives; experiences which they made valuable use of for the benefit of others. The most important fact relating to these famous personalities, however, is that they did not TRY and develop psychic powers. They concentrated, always, in doing God's Will by earnest prayer. Their unexpected contact with the spirit world through visions or conversations with spiritual beings was always welcome, but not specifically sought. Daily 'seeking' through prayer for guidance, inspiration and strength is a 'must' for all aspiring mediums, and those who may find themselves unexpectedly involved.

Finally we should examine our understanding of the subject with another question: 'Why does mediumship interest me?'. It is the answer to this question which will govern the degree of usefulness that this book may have for the individual reader, who has shown a degree of interest by reading this far.

One thing is certain, however; there is nothing in the extremely unselfconscious story of Stan Walsh's mediumship that misinterprets the subject. Just as Walsh was a great medium, bringing down needed knowledge, solace and wisdom from high sources, so this book can become a medium for the reader, bringing into his or her life new knowledge of what mediumship is about—and the absolute conviction of the certainty of Eternity.

2

THE ACHILLES HEEL OF SPIRITUALISM

For there is hope of a tree, if it be cut down, that it will sprout again

BOOK OF JOB

It was under the banner of Spiritualism that Stan Walsh began his mediumship and developed the early stages of his gift of deep-trance mediumship. He abandoned this religion later, however, at the request of his high spiritual guides.

These guiding spiritual personalities, speaking through Walsh's lips, told his followers that they must no longer call themselves 'Spiritualists' because the name was being degraded by unworthy and false mediums.

The followers of Stan Walsh were to henceforth call themselves simply, 'followers of the truth of God'.

It was explained that, while there were still many sincere and devout people worshipping God in its name and honest mediums still associated with Spiritualism, these were in the minority.

Spiritualism had been launched many years before by mediums who sincerely desired to bring comfort to the bereaved, without any thought of monetary gain. It gained the blessing and cooperation of highly progressed spiritual entities who assisted in the advance of the movement and in the development of the gifts of its genuine mediums.

Thus, in those early years, the name of Spiritualism was respected and it did a great deal of good for its loyal followers on earth and also for those who needed prayers and help in their efforts to progress spiritually on the other side of that 'barrier' we call death.

Unfortunately, as the years went on a host of new mediums encroached on the movement; many unworthy or improperly motivated mediums among them. The high standard of the work of Spiritualism was reduced; it lost respect as it lost touch with its original pure motives. Eventually the desire to give comfort and hope to the sorrowing without monetary return was regarded as unbusinesslike. False or weak mediums and charlatans whose real motives were financial gain, began to infiltrate into the once respected churches of the movement. They began to impose upon the credulous and play upon the foolishness of weak minds, thus bringing the name of Spiritualism into ridicule and contempt in many quarters.

I verified this for myself when, in the course of research, I visited many churches and centres of Spiritualism both here in Australia and abroad. In the experience of lecturing on many platforms and deliberately seeking out mediums from whom I obtained a variety of spiritual messages, some sincere and others very much less than sincere, I formed an opinion that the direction of Walsh's spirit guides was well justified. In both London and Australia, where I did most of my research, there was far too much activity that was mercenary and inefficient and should not have been operating in the name of spiritual truth. I had discussions with a number of Spiritualist church officers who sincerely deplored the downgrade in mediumistic ability and their commercial trends.

In a speech given at a spiritual congress in Copenhagen some years ago, Mr Ralph Rossiter, the then secretary of the Spiritualists Association of Great Britain, said, 'Undoubtedly the standard of mediumship is important and there are far too many undeveloped mediums invited to our platforms'.

Because of our fallible natures we will always have fortune tellers, genuine and false, to satisfy the natural curiosity of our minds as to what is going to happen to us in the future, but these soothsayers, good and bad, should not be associated under any circumstances with the true name of Spiritualism.

These professional fortune tellers, including cup-readers, palm-readers and card-readers, who work under the name of Spiritualism—and usually for financial gain—have always been, and always will be, the 'Achilles Heel' of this movement.

THE ACHILLES HEEL OF SPIRITUALISM

Sir James Barrie used to tell a quaint story of an old charwoman who 'wished that she was Queen Victoria, so that she could ring a bell at any time, night or morning, and order boiled beef and cabbage'.

There are too many mediums who develop, or try to develop, psychic gifts, not so much to give proof or clearer understanding of the afterlife, but to be able to tell fortunes to all and sundry—often at substantial fees.

These neglect the high and noble calling of true followers of Spiritualism—that is to demonstrate the truth of life after death. These people demean themselves by reducing great gifts of the spirit to the 'boiled beef and cabbage' level.

There is a distinct difference between fortune telling and prophesying.

Most fortune tellers practise for financial reward, although some do use genuine psychic gifts for other reasons—to entertain, to please friends, to guide people towards prosperity, success, etc. and even in the cause of psychic science. Unfortunately the majority have no other object in mind than an easy way to earn money. Even when their psychic gifts are genuine and their motives fair, they make no reference to the 'hereafter' or effort to use their power to give messages to their listener from loved ones in the spirit world or even to produce proof that these loved ones still 'live'. This is, of course, because of the type of listener for whom they cater—people not interested in contacting the 'departed' or obtaining spiritual guidance which will help them to progress in love of their fellow man and understanding of God's universal plan for creation. These people seek to learn about what lies ahead of them in this life in the way of good fortune, health, human relationships, etc.

A genuine, truly gifted medium uses his or her psychic abilities to bring down spiritual knowledge and messages from departed friends and relations to his followers. The chief aim is to give spiritual comfort and assurance to listeners and to prove that loved ones who have passed on really do still 'live'. Mediums strive to make themselves perfect instruments for communication between the spirit world and this physical world. Prophesying is usually an integral part of this communication. The medium's part is to describe and give the names of these spiritual relatives and friends and also to relay advice, given by the latter, to the listener.

Often the advice refers to something that is going to happen to the listener and it is here that prophesying is made.

The medium may see the spirit form of the listener's mother standing beside him, or her, and proceeds to give the mother's name and describe her appearance to the listener. It is natural that the mother in spirit, having fourth dimensional vision, should tell the listener of future events which are important to their lives. This part of the mother's message is 'personal prophesying'. The essential difference between this and fortune telling is that the medium does not seek this information on behalf of the client or listener; the medium is merely the instrument whereby someone in the spirit world communicates the information directly to the person they feel should be informed. The second difference, usually applicable, is that the motive for fortune telling is material gain and the motive for prophesying via a medium is a genuine desire to inspire, guide or help someone.

The vital difference between the two is beginning to be recognized by sincere followers and exponents of Spiritualism today and through their firm and prayerful influence this important movement is being slowly and gradually cleansed of the bad name it acquired a generation ago. All over the world it is being renewed under new banners and worthy leaders.

The story of Stan Walsh's development could not have been written without this frank commentary on his connections with Spiritualism and the reasons for his disassociation with it. It is hoped that the very frankness of this report will act to help the movement that gave him so much inspiring friendship and encouragement in the early stages of his mediumship—help it return to the strength and pure standing that it once held. As this story unfolds the reader will meet many wonderful adherents of Spiritualism, such as Mrs Beames and others whose faith and enthusiasm imbued this remarkable medium with the confidence to continue his spiritual progression.

3

AN UNCOMPLICATED MAN

There are rare men who seem under a vow of happiness

Anon

In an address to the Australian Institute of Management, a noted Federal Cabinet Minister remarked: 'In the public mind all improvements made in our national development are planned only by Government. This is not always so. Often we should thank private individuals for such improvements'.

This piece of wisdom applies equally to the spiritual or religious life of our community. Frequently it is the layman or private person who is responsible for the most exciting developments in our spiritual progression. An unknown individual is often the means for unusual revelations which may throw new light on orthodox opinions.

Such a person was Stan Walsh—the most remarkable and yet the most uncomplicated man I have ever met.

Born in 1891 in the Victorian country town of Ararat, young Walsh moved to the city of Melbourne when he and his four brothers and two sisters were still quite young. He thought of himself always as a Melbournian and it was here that he lived out his life, never travelling abroad or spending more than brief holidays interstate. He never married and remained living in the family home with his parents and one unmarried sister, Norma throughout his adult life.

He had a normal primary school education and did not go on to secondary school, but entered the work force as soon as he was legally eligible to begin a trade. Carpentry was that trade and he followed it all his life.

Stan Walsh was always a very contented and happy man. He enjoyed his family life which was simple, solid and Anglican. He liked the simple things of life; gardening, the company of good friends, occasional weekends in the country. He was small in stature, slim and slightly built as a young man but more filled out later. The only striking feature about him was his large, shining, dark brown eyes—and they were unforgettable! His other facial features were unimportant, although there was a suggestion of sensitivity and a faint suggestion of 'prunes and prisms' about his lips.

He was always rather staid in his personal appearance with a carefully knotted tie, well pressed trousers and immaculately polished shoes, but his manner was unassuming and he was very gentle and utterly sincere.

His first psychic experience occurred when he was about twelve years old and a choirboy at St. Lukes Church of England in Dorcas Street, South Melbourne. One Sunday morning, during the service, he saw what he called 'angels without wings' coming down through the stained glass windows and the roof into the church. To him they appeared to be robed in brilliant white light and looked very beautiful.

He confided what he saw to one or two of the choirboys who laughed and said he must have dreamt it. But young Walsh stoutly denied that he was asleep. 'I saw them when I was singing—so how could I have been asleep?' he defended.

The vicar heard about it. 'Are you sure it was not imagination?' he asked. 'No, sir, they were there, I saw them.' Walsh was most emphatic! 'Well' said the Vicar, 'if you say you really saw them, I believe you, but I advise you to keep it to yourself. Visions from God's Kingdom are too sacred to be told to all and sundry!' I was attracted to Stan Walsh from the first time we met. He impressed me, not only as a medium, but also as a man. As time went on and I entered more and more into his private life, my respect for him deepened. I could trust him implicitly. He was, indeed, the most uncomplicated man I had ever met. There was nothing artificial in his nature. He was always just himself; quiet, shy and completely without guile.

He loved life and he loved people. He took great joy in pouring out his thoughts of simple things to responsive ears; the favourite flowers in his garden, his dog, his family, antiques, a good play or musical comedy. He spoke rapidly and artlessly, very much like an enthusiastic schoolboy describing the fish he caught or the games he played.

He was not an intellectual. He had the usual state school education, starting work at a box making factory when he was fifteen; but he learnt much from life and people. He was more than a deep-trance medium, he was a modern prophet; but he was not perfect—just an everyday human being with the usual little faults inherent in us all. However, he had a very simple faith in God, and that was important. It took a little while before he realised that faith in God applies, not only to Sunday, but on every day of the week.

He had his fair share of common sense and a keen sense of humour; two things that protected him from getting a swelled head or an exaggerated opinion of himself when, in later years, he was surrounded by a host of admiring followers and their never ending praise and adulation. As Emerson puts it: 'The less a man thinks or knows about his virtues the better we like him'. Walsh was just such a man.

Through him, I, together with many others, actually 'communed with the Saints'—and a host of Saints in the making! He was the mouthpiece for many Biblical personalities who spoke and taught through him, and who were the means of changing the lives, beliefs and unbeliefs of several hundred people over the years of his mission.

These Bible personalities, or 'high guides' as we called them, proved a stumbling block to some. They acknowledged that his gifts were genuine, but refused to believe that high spiritual entities such as John the Baptist, King David, Samuel, John the Most Beloved, Mary Magdalene, Joan of Arc and a host of others known and unknown to past generations could, or would, speak through such an ordinary, almost unlettered man as Walsh.

Adorning the altar of the Capuchin Church is Murillo's masterpiece: Madonna of the Napkin. He was too poor to buy a canvas, so painted it on a kitchen napkin thrown to him by the cook. And in the Uffizi Gallery in Florence is Raphael's *Madonna della Sedia* painted on the lid of a wine cask! Those who doubted that the Saints spoke through Walsh forgot one thing; that God invariably chooses the meek and lowly, the humble and not-so-clever to be the mouthpiece for His revelations—human beings as ordinary as an old napkin or the lid of a wine cask.

It has always been so.

4

A GIFT ACCEPTED

Gifts come from high in their own peculiar forms

GOETHE

In 1919 Walsh made friends with an actor working in the J. C. Williamson Theatres. His name was Billy Ladd. Ladd took his new friend back stage and introduced him to a variety of theatrical personalities; this to Walsh's intense delight.

Then death intruded into Walsh's life for the first time. Billy Ladd died suddenly. At the funeral Walsh broke down and wept. Later, an unexpected incident brought back to mind a certain detail of that painful scene.

Some months later Stan Walsh met a bread carter called Herbert Jones.

Jones was a sun-tanned, stocky man with a soft heart and a sentimental nature carefully camouflaged by a grim face and a blunt and forthright way of speaking. This call-a-spade-a-spade manner was to be very helpful to Walsh later on when awkward situations arose which could only be solved by a plain speaking friend.

Despite the disparity in their natures and years (Jones was much older than his friend) these two simple minded men soon became firm friends—a friendship that was to last for over twenty years.

God often uses human beings as instruments to influence a man or woman to move in a certain direction without that person realising it.

The flowering of the first gift of deep-trance to come to Walsh had to be accomplished in an atmosphere most conducive to its development, which was the séance room of the Spiritualists.

Jones was the instrument, in this case, to guide Walsh towards this atmosphere. Jones was interested in Spiritualism; Walsh was not—definitely not! But the stolid, imperturbable Jones was patient and persistent, and eventually wore down his friend's resistance.

The result was that one Sunday afternoon Jones steered Walsh towards a Spiritualistic church in Richmond. It was there that his favourite medium and friend, Mrs Beames used to demonstrate. She was a plump, jolly-faced matron, well known and respected in spiritualistic circles of those days. She was known in spiritual circles as a semi-trance medium. Her 'guide' was a one-time Indian chief called 'Wagga'. He was her spiritual protector, or doorkeeper. Spirits could not speak through her lips without his permission.

The attendance of these two young men at the church was not an auspicious start for the sceptical Walsh. Some of the incidents at the meeting left him confused. He could not understand how spirit forces could use the lips of another person.

After the meeting they walked up to Bridge Road to catch the tram. Jones tried to explain to his friend what was meant by 'semi-trance'. Walsh shook his head. 'I still don't understand it.' While waiting for the tram, they strolled over to a furniture shop window and stared at the contents, Jones still trying to make him understand, but Walsh shook his head again. 'It's all very odd to me', he said. They boarded the tram still arguing. In the city, before they each departed for their homes, Jones said, 'What about coming to one of her séances at her Port Melbourne home?' Walsh refused, but the irrepressible Jones persisted, and finally extracted a promise from his friend that he would go with Jones the following Tuesday night.

So they went. Jones knocked at the door and Mrs Beames appeared. At the sight of Walsh she smiled rather grimly. 'Are you sure you want to come in, young man? My guide, Wagga, told me what you said when you were looking in that furniture shop window— that it was 'all very odd'. We are not odd I can assure you.' Walsh looked sheepish and rather startled. Mrs Beames' awareness of what he said to his friend in a deserted street in Richmond staggered him, 'I'm sorry, Mrs Beames, if I offended you.' Mrs Beames laughed. 'All right, youngster, you can come in this time; perhaps we can make you think otherwise.' Inside, Walsh was very subdued. He sat down feeling nervous and uncomfortable, still puzzling in his mind how Mrs Beames knew what he said.

Up to this time young Walsh had not the slightest knowledge, inclination nor understanding of Spiritualism, but all this was to be changed sooner than he thought. Within two weeks a psychic thunderbolt struck him and changed his whole conception of the movement, and, indeed, the whole trend of his future life.

The séance began; first with a prayer and then a hymn. Mrs Beames then stood up and, under strong inspiration from Wagga, gave messages and advice to the sitters. The séance lasted a little over an hour. At the end of it Walsh found himself completely forgiven. Mrs Beames was mollified by his nervously uttered, 'Thanks for letting me stay'. She asked him how he liked it. 'Very much', 'but my hands—they kept shaking and trembling! I couldn't control them.' Mrs Beames smiled. 'That sounds promising, Sonny. Come again next week. Bring a pencil and writing pad with you, and let us see what happens.' Next week he came along again—more at ease. During the séance Mrs Beames told him to hold the pencil and pad on his lap and see what happened. The séance was almost half over when suddenly his right hand began to write on the paper; writing furiously as if controlled by some invisible hand. Later, when the lights were turned up he found himself possessor of a sheaf of written messages for every member of the circle.

They were all delighted, particularly Mrs Beames. 'You are an automatic writer, young man. You have a fine gift, cultivate it!' Then came the third week. At the first meeting he almost had to be dragged there by his indefatigable friend. Now he was completely converted, and keen to see what would happen next with his writing pad.

He sat in his place in the circle, pad on knee, pencil poised, like a stenographer ready to take down dictation from an invisible executive.

The séance commenced. Lights were dimmed. There was the usual prayer and hymn—and then it happened.

Walsh, for the first time in his life, experienced a complete blackout! 'It was just as if I had fainted', he said. When he came to, dazed and sleepy, he found himself surrounded by his excited companions. He was told that after the hymn had been sung, a hoarse cry came from his throat; the pad and pencil were thrown into the air, and he was completely controlled by a Red Indian, who began to talk excitedly in deep guttural tones, and in a foreign language; later they learnt it was in the Red Indian's native tongue.

This went on for a while and then Mrs Beames asked the Indian to try and speak in 'our tongue'. The guide paused, and then began to speak slowly in broken English. He said his name was Malocca. He had been sent by God to be the chief guide and doorkeeper to young Walsh. There was much for him to do.

Then Malocca allowed other spirit entities to speak through Walsh and to different ones in the room, including Jones and Mrs Beames. Everyone was able to recognize the names given and the messages sent.

All this was later related to Walsh by a buzzing bunch of excited people, all talking at once. Walsh stared at them in amazement. Had they all gone mad? What was all this talk about deep-trance? He must have fainted. He couldn't remember anything. 'If I were in a dead faint, how could I walk around and give messages when I was unconscious?' he asked.

Mrs Beames chipped in and tried to explain to him that under deep-trance the instrument is controlled and knows nothing about what is going on. Walsh still found it hard to believe until Jones spoke to him. He told his bewildered friend that there was a message for him from his erstwhile friend, Billy Ladd. Said Jones: 'Billy said that the day he was buried, and before the coffin lid was closed, you secretly dropped a bunch of violets, his favourite flowers, into the coffin. Is that right?' Then Walsh was convinced. 'That's true! I never told a soul about that!' 'You are a very lucky chap, Sonny,' said Mrs Beames. 'Very few people ever gain the gift of deep-trance. You will have to get used to the idea of saying and doing things that you don't know anything about.' It was a strange experience for Walsh, and it took a few weeks before he could get used to the idea.

And so, at the age of twenty, Stan Walsh commenced a ministry that was to last for many years—a ministry that was to bring joy and happiness to a host of people, both in this world, and in the lower planes of the spirit world.

5

THE UNIVERSITY OF EXPERIENCE

Only God can make a silk purse out of a sow's ear

Anon

When a great spiritual force descends upon a human mortal without warning, it sometimes turns out that the real significance of this spiritual gift, for the time being, is not altogether understood by the recipient.

Such was the case with Walsh in the early stages of his development. He was in a great state of suppressed excitement and very proud of this unexpected gift thrown into his lap.

In the twinkling of an eye he found himself a local celebrity—a deep-trance medium; and this power, said Mrs Beames, was as rare as comets. He found himself the centre of an admiring crowd, her crowd. She began to take second place among her followers; she was only an inspirational medium. She being human, was not altogether pleased, so after a month or so they mutually agreed to separate. They parted with expressions of goodwill on both sides. Walsh promised to continue to help her, however, at the services of her Richmond Church.

At the invitation of a Mrs Lehman he began to hold meetings at her place in Canterbury Road, Albert Park. He couldn't hold them at his own place as his parents had no knowledge of Spiritualism, and didn't understand it. They were staunch Church of England adherents. The result was that they never really understood the exact nature of their son's psychic activities. He was their favourite boy and the only worry they attached to him was 'this trance business', as his mother expressed it to me once. Stan did not discuss it with them. 'I find it impossible to explain it to Mum or Dad', he told me. They just would not understand it.' I knew how he felt. What we do not understand we frequently either fear or dislike. His parents feared this gift of his because it was something hard to fathom. However, as the years went on, various followers of Stan, who visited their home, including myself, were able to assure them that their son was doing a great amount of good with his trance gift, and they were satisfied.

The only members of these first meetings at Mrs Lehman's were Walsh, Jones, Mrs Lehman, Mrs Martin, a friend of the latter, and a school teacher, Miss Mabel Grenville. The séances were held on a Tuesday. On Sundays Walsh assisted at Mrs Beames' Richmond services; but apart from these commitments, the two complacent young men considered they had their own private monopoly of fortune telling. It opened up a new world for them, a world of comfortable armchairs, rich rewards and a perpetual chorus of praise and adulation from admirers. They dreamt of world travel with Jones as the business manager, Walsh as the star; a snug and comfortable existence; and rich clients eagerly seeking to have their fortunes told at satisfactory fees.

The spiritual citizens that had so suddenly dropped in on them from the spirit world were free from time and space. They came from the Eternal Now, so that everything was revealed to their ethereal gaze—yesterday, today and tomorrow were as one. They could see into the future! Therefore, apart from these meetings and services at Mrs Beames' and other Spiritualistic churches, they held their own private two-man meetings at Jones' private home in Crown Street, Newmarket. His mother lived with him, a tiny rosy faced, white haired, little woman—over ninety, but still sprightly, forthright and alert. She looked askance at these little meetings held in her dining room. 'Talking to those spirits will drive you out of your mind', she would snap.

The procedure was always the same. A list of questions would be made out by Jones; questions for which he and Walsh sought answers, such as: 'Will I stay in my present job? Will Stan ever give up work and travel? Will I ever marry? Will Stan? Will Stan's sister's boy friend marry her? Will I or Stan ever come into money?' These and other questions were asked of Malocca and various relatives in the spirit world who controlled Walsh.

Malocca must have had amazing patience in those days. Bert told me that Malocca used to answer the reasonable questions, and leave unanswered questions of a gross material nature. Later, spirits from a lower plane than Malocca's answered their material questions and for a while led these young men along the wrong path—the path of gross fortune telling.

Stan, also told me an amusing incident at one of these early two-man séances at Bert's home. Bert Jones, in spite of his keen interest in Spiritualism was a very irritating 'doubting Thomas'. Where spirit messages were concerned he would not trust his own mother without absolute proof! He did not trust his best friend either, Stan told me. He had to have definite proof. At one of these 'at home' séances, Walsh was controlled by a spirit. When he came to full consciousness again, Jones explained to him who it was. He said it was his (Jones') father. This was the first of his relatives to come back and speak to him from the other side of life. Said Jones: 'If you really are my father could you talk to me in Welsh like you used to at times?' His father complied convincingly. 'Now would you mind singing to me in Welsh—the favourite song you used to sing to Mum?' His father again obliged. Then Jones asked his father what was his last word before he left the body; his father told him, and also other intimate family secrets. So Jones was satisfied it was his father. 'I should think you ought to be', grumbled Walsh, when later told what happened.

After a few months Malocca insisted that they cease having these two-man séances, tactfully suggesting that it was too much of a strain on the instrument. Round about this time Walsh developed the inspirational gifts of clairaudience and clairvoyance.

Jones often went to the races, Walsh very rarely. When Walsh developed the new gifts, Jones suggested they could, perhaps, find out the name of winning horses before the races were run. For a while, Walsh, young and thoughtless, agreed. What they did not realise then was that by seeking to gain material knowledge from the spirit world with a view to financial gain, they would inevitably draw towards them 'earth bound' spirits.

It is perhaps necessary at this stage to explain, in brief, what is meant by 'earth bound' spirits. To spiritualists it means exactly what it says—that this type of spirit is 'earth bound'. On earth, this type of spirit had led an evil life. When they passed into the spirit world they found themselves dwelling in an atmosphere of darkness—a darkness of their own making.

Having no desire to rise to higher spheres, that is, to better themselves, they would try to get away from this darkness by keeping close to the earth, where they lived when in the flesh. While on this earth they may have been, perhaps, inveterate gamblers, alcoholics, drug addicts, thieves, confidence men, sex perverts, people who deliberately and selfishly hurt others and/or themselves. Deprived of their fleshly bodies they, nevertheless, enjoyed the vicarious excitement of hovering around their favourite haunts—racecourses, hotels, places of ill repute, gambling resorts, and so on.

As explained previously, once a spirit passes into the etheric spheres there is no time nor space—just the eternal Now—so that ALL spirits, strong or weak, can see into the future.

These earth-bound spirits, sometimes known as 'unprogressed', are, therefore, only interested in human mortals who have the same inclinations that they had on earth. Like calls to like.

We know, from what we were taught by the guides, that a peculiar light shines from the soul of all mediums, no matter what their gift may be. This light is either dull or bright, according to the moral fibre and character of the medium in question. As all mediums constitute some form of 'doorway' between the two worlds, this peculiar light is an indicator to the inhabitants of the spirit world that through these mediums there is an opportunity to once again contact the world of flesh. Thus, if the character or disposition of any medium is grossly material or worldly they draw towards them earth-bound spirits who share their weakness. In like manner, mediums with characters beyond reproach—selfless and dedicated to helping their fellow men—draw only the progressed or better type of spirits into their lives.

It can thus be seen that the tendency developed by Jones and Walsh to seek financial gain at the racecourses would draw towards them these unhappy spirits who would eagerly impress Walsh's mind with the names of horses they could see would win in future events.

This aroused the wrath of Malocca and other guides of high standing who were helping with the development of Walsh's gifts for much higher purposes. Their inordinate love of money had drawn ugly conditions into the séance room. Malocca in an open meeting appealed to Jones to discard these foolish dreams and to pray earnestly to be guided only by God's will and to consecrate their lives and their gifts to help others less fortunate than themselves. The other members of the class heartily agreed. Walsh was told after the meeting what had been said and was deeply impressed.

He and Jones determined from then on to concentrate only on the spiritual.

Unfortunately the spirit is willing, but sometimes caught napping.

About a month later Walsh was invited to a race meeting with a party which included a well known inspirational medium. Walsh, carried away by the excitement of the race crowd, forgot his good intentions. The lady with psychic ability gaily suggested that she and Walsh between them pick the winners using their mediumistic gifts for this purpose. Walsh thoughtlessly agreed.

First she held the race book and 'concentrated'. 'That will be the winner' she said. It was! Then it was Walsh's turn. He, too, using his psychic gift, was able to divine the winner. This went on all day, and they won on every race.

Jones would have nothing to do with their forecasts. 'Not for me', he declared, 'you know Malocca warned you about using your gifts wrongly.

You'll get into trouble over this.' So Jones lost on the day, using his own judgement, but although light in pocket, he was satisfied. 'Anyhow, my conscience is clear', he said, rather piously.

That same night was their weekly meeting at Mrs Lehman's home.

Malocca came through and sternly denounced his instrument. He said that the latter, through his disobedience and flagrant use of his spiritual gifts for unworthy purposes, had drawn into the room unclean and evil conditions. He went on to say that there were two lost souls (earthbound spirits) in the room. It was these two actual spirits that had given Walsh the information of the racehorse winners that day.

Malocca explained that he and other guides did not want these two spirits to leave without trying to help them. The only way to do this was to let them control the instrument and speak to the sitters. He appealed to the sitters not to be upset by the behaviour of these two, but to extend to them the warm hand of friendship and tell them they would try and help the visitors with their prayers. He added that these two unfortunate people when on this earth were outcasts and friendless and that the sincere sympathy and love of human beings could do more to help them at their present stage than high angels in heaven.

Malocca then withdrew and allowed these two strangers to take turns in controlling the instrument.

The first one was a man. To the horror of the sitters he swore and cursed and threw the medium on the ground screaming and yelling. Eventually Jones and the others were able to persuade him to calm down. Slowly he obeyed and allowed Jones to put him back quietly on the chair. They asked him what his name was. He said, Wally. They told him he was very welcome and they would try and help him as much as possible with their loving thoughts and prayers to progress to happier planes. He eventually left much calmer and happier than when he came. Walsh came to consciousness, panting and gasping—and aching from head to foot.

Malocca then came through again and explained that this man, on earth, had become an alcoholic and had died in a raving delirium. As soon as his spirit touched the human body he brought that condition into the medium. The violent strain he had placed on Walsh's body was not intentional. Wally was sorry. 'Pray for him' added Malocca. 'Don't condemn him. Your prayers will help us to lift him out of the darkness in which he dwells.' The members of the circle immediately prayed earnestly for Wally. But Walsh's troubles were not yet over. A little later Malocca said that there was the spirit of a woman in the room in a state of despair, and degradation.

Malocca announced she too must be helped. Pray for her. Let her see you are her friend. Try and make her understand you want to help her and that you love her. No matter how low she has fallen, she is one of God's children and must be helped. Again Malocca left the body and then with frenzied violence the spirit of this woman came through. She demanded a drink, and when it was not forthcoming, cursed and abused the sitters.

Jones tried to make her understand that he and his friends wanted to help her. She refused to listen, and in her rage she rolled Walsh on the floor, screaming and cursing, and yelling for a drink. The trembling sitters prayed hard that God would send light into her soul. Gradually she began to calm down. They asked her what her name was and where she lived on the earth. She said she was known as Mother Meldrum and that she lived in the slum section of North Melbourne. She had been a confirmed alcoholic. They promised to help her with their prayers and kindly thoughts, and at last they were able to persuade her to leave the medium.

The whole night had been taken up with these two unhappy souls.

Malocca, in closing the meeting, said that they would be taken care of by the high spiritual guides and helped on the road of progression.

Finally Malocca warned them that if Walsh continued to use the gift God had given him for mercenary purposes, he would eventually lose it altogether.

When the exhausted Walsh came to after the séance he was in a state bordering on collapse. He was trembling from head to foot and the others were visibly shaken.

'Never again', said Mrs Martin, jumping to her feet, 'that's the last time I'll come to these meetings Stan, if you continue to use your gifts, for picking winners. I agree with Malocca. The work is too sacred for that. I could never stand another meeting like that, it was awful.' Both Miss Grenville and Mrs Lehman emphatically agreed.

'You don't have to tell me', murmured the trembling Stan. 'Never again. I've learnt my lesson. I've been a fool.' So far it seemed that the spiritual powers so generously bestowed upon him had only produced a 'sow's ear'. But Walsh, as previously explained, was just an ordinary, honest working man, equipped with just an average education. He was a good clean living young man, but up to this stage incapable of properly understanding and appreciating what his mission really was in life.

The raw material that the guides had to work upon in those early days was rather crude, but they could see something far deeper and nobler lying latent in the hearts of these two young men.

They knew that, slowly but surely, God would prune away these unlovely features and ultimately produce 'the silk purse' that He was fashioning in their hearts.

6

SPIRITUAL TEACHERS

Faith is nothing more than obedience

VOLTAIRE

Up to now the weekly meetings at Mrs Lehman's had been the usual placid, run-of-the-mill séances. But the advent of the disruptive elements referred to in the last chapter wrought gradual changes.

Walsh found himself undergoing uncomfortable self examinations. He realised he had a lot to learn; that he was not worthy of the gifts so generously given to him. He had received, not only the gifts of deep-trance, but also clairaudience and clairvoyance. In addition he was blessed with loyal friends whose prayers, faith and steadfast support never failed him.

All these precious pearls cast at his feet were his! And yet he had an uneasy feeling that he was, perhaps without thinking, treading some of them underfoot through his inclination at times to use these gifts for material purposes. He inwardly vowed that this must stop. He determined to make a mental right-about-face. From henceforth he would obey Malocca and his helpers implicitly.

Round about this time, for family reasons, Mrs Lehman had to move to the country. Mrs Martin promptly invited the others to continue these weekly meetings at her home, also in Albert Park. It was there that each one of the remaining four gave a solemn promise to Malocca that they would, from then onward, seek only the highest and best. Obedience to the teachings of the guide was to be their watchword. This was the beginning of the Inner Circle.

Walsh and Jones sometimes faltered and made mistakes, but these were less and less frequent and were always quickly rectified. A novice monk once asked St Benedict, 'Father, what is your definition of a Saint?' St Benedict replied, simply: 'A saint, my son, is a person who never stops trying'.

Walsh at this time began the habit of mental prayer. The instigation of this practice was part of his development and instructions were given to him clairaudiently by his guides. He was advised to take time to pray for strength and stability in all that he did. As a result he never ceased trying, nor did the others—and they were all continually encouraged by very highly evolved guides who now commenced to come down from higher planes of the spiritual world.

Thus the amazing spiritual powers that gradually built up over the years within this Inner Circle were the result of this earnest and steadfast dedication of each member to bring the Truth of God into the hearts of all who were invited in subsequent years to their gatherings.

The first of the spiritual personalities to come down from higher planes was Angus Du Font, a former Frenchman, and Professor Jenkinson, who had lived in England.

Walsh first became aware of the proximity of the former when coming home one night from work. Walking along Albert Park Road he suddenly heard an inward voice say: 'Next Sunday you will lecture at Mrs Beames' church. Later he discovered that the voice he heard was this French guide.

This unexpected message from the unseen world was not altogether welcomed by Walsh. In those early days he had never stood upon a public platform as a deep trance-medium to lecture. He was extremely nervous and shy and the idea of giving a public exhibition of his gifts terrified him.

He was quite positive that he would not be able to do it.

That Sunday afternoon when he entered the Rotherwood St Church in Richmond, Mrs Beames approached him and stated that she had been impressed by 'Wagga', her guide, to ask Walsh to give an address. The reluctant Walsh tried to stammer a refusal, but was benevolently hustled on to the platform with Mrs Beames and several other mediums. He was in a confused state of mind and stared nervously at the sea of smiling faces looking up at him. At last he plucked up enough courage to whisper to her that he had no intention of lecturing. His refusal was met with a sweet smile and a nod of the head from Mrs Beames. Then came the opening prayer and a hymn after which the smiling leader stood up and blandly announced, to Walsh's consternation, that they would now be addressed by Mr Walsh under deep-trance.

Walsh shook his head vigorously and that was all he remembered.

When he regained consciousness he heard the leader thanking him for giving a most interesting lecture by a new guide called Angus Du Font.

After they left the church, Walsh asked Herb Jones what the lecture was like. The forthright Herb sniffed, 'The lecture was all right, but you wouldn't keep still. You gradually began to turn away from the audience until you nearly had your back towards them. I was in a sweat and kept on saying to myself: "Turn him round, Malocca, turn him round". Slowly you turned round again to face the audience, but I was glad when it was all over.

Later on Malocca explained to Jones that it was the first time Du Font had tried to control a human instrument since he passed over; in addition, it was the first time that his instrument, Walsh, had lectured in public.

The subconscious effect of these two factors made it difficult for the guide to control the body completely. This slight fault would disappear with practice.

From then onward Du Font came regularly to the Inner Circle to teach and instruct them on the spiritual life and the spiritual world. His first talk was a brief life history of himself, just before he passed over. On this occasion Miss Grenville took down notes of what he said.

Du Font said it was forty-seven years ago, by our time, since he passed into the spirit world. His aim now, after 'years' of study and progression in the higher spheres, was to teach others about life after death. What we on the earth world called 'death' was actually a door, through which the human spirit leaves the physical body and enters into its spiritual home or mansion.

Before he crossed into the spirit world he did not believe in immortality or spirit return. He was an Intellectual and a Rationalist. To him, belief in eternal life was utter nonsense, He did not believe in God. He had been well educated and had developed a gift of eloquence which he had put to wrong use. Through this gift he turned many people away from their church and their God.

One night after returning home from one of these anti-religious lectures he opened the front door and was confronted with a vision of his mother, who had died some years before, standing in front of him, gazing at him sadly.

He tried to put her lovely image out of his mind as mere fancy, but all night he felt as if she were watching him. In the morning he awoke with a deep feeling within his heart that something was wrong. Could he have been mistaken in his loudly reiterated views? In any case, he decided to abandon any further lectures on the subject.

A few months later he had an opportunity of finding out for himself what was the Truth. He became very ill and realised he was dying; he was terrified. Then the spirit of his mother appeared to him again, and the fear that had gripped him seemed to melt away.

He felt as if his spirit was leaving the body—then—a moment of utter darkness, which suddenly lifted, and there was his mother, real and beautiful. She took him by the hand and with reassuring words led him into a new world—a world of light.

His first feeling, when he was aware of what had happened, was as if he had returned from a long journey and was home again. Relatives and friends, who had gone before, were there to meet him, and then his mother conveyed him to the spiritual mansion which had been built for him but really by himself.

In this 'home' he saw representations of everything he had done in his earth life, from the beginning to the end. Every word, thought or deed, good or bad, was registered in some extraordinary way on the ethereal walls of this home. No matter how small the deed, word or thought—there they were! Clearly noted or marked down! As he gazed in astonishment at his past life revealed all around him he began to understand, after deep reflection, that God does not judge a deed by the time or money spent on it, nor does he judge us by what we have said—good, bad, or indifferent. He judges us by the actual THOUGHT that prompted us in whatever we did, or said.

Those events which he had thought were of greatest importance in his life, were, in many cases, hardly noted at all; but many little deeds, kind words or thoughts, which he had completely forgotten, were shown up in the form of beautiful flowers. These were the things regarded by God as important.

Around these walls there appeared here and there darkened shadows.

Peering into these he discerned the things which were wrong in God's sight; and among these shadows was one in which he was himself lecturing on the platform bringing doubt and unbelief into the hearts of his listeners.

This realisation that he was the means of turning so many away from the Truth brought sorrow to his soul. He wanted to make amends. He wanted to go back to the earth right away and try and work upon the minds of those he had led astray, and bring back the Truth into their hearts.

But his mother, whose unexpected appearance just before he died, had changed his outlook on death, and who had bridged the river of death for him, said he had to remember that God was, above all things, just and merciful. One is not judged by the day but by the whole life. The good he had performed in other ways outweighed the harm he had done in his latter days. His mother told him that one day he might be permitted to return to earth to help others, but it would be wise for him to progress first in the world of spirit. From then onward he sought, like many others with him, to learn as much as possible from these angelic teachers which came down from higher planes of light. From them he gained knowledge and wisdom far greater than anything he had learnt on earth.

Angus Du Font then went on to give his hearers a brief description of the world of spirit. He said it comprised many spheres of light. Nothing of a material nature existed there. The beauty and the scenery were indescribable and there is nothing on earth that can compare with it.

There are eleven spheres or planes of light. The first plane dwells in darkness, but with each succeeding plane more light appears. We pass over from the world of man to one of these planes, according to the life we have lived, and from then onward, progress to higher planes according to our own individual desires. Eventually every soul reaches the Eleventh Plane of Light, and from there, will merge into the great Light of God.

Du Font concluded by saying that he would tell them more of this world as time went on; he would visit their room often. That was the first of many talks given by this guide over the years.

The second teacher, Professor Jenkinson, also came into their midst round about this time, and began to teach them likewise. On one occasion Miss Grenville asked if he could give them any information about his earth life. He promised to do so later.

That night before retiring Walsh was impressed to take pen and pencil, and there, sitting on the edge of his bed, was impelled by an unseen hand to record details of the life of Professor Jenkinson who was born on June 21,1811. He was the son of the Carl of Chichester, the honoured President of the Church Missionary Society of that year. The Jenkinsons had lived at Norwich for many years and were celebrated for their great zeal in the promotion of the spiritual interests of their countrymen. In the time of Edward I, the family was in possession of a Lordship at Pelham in Herefordshire. Jenkinson was brought up at Stanmore, not far from Brighton and was educated at Westminster. At Christchurch, Oxford, he took his degree as B.A. in 1834. Three years later he was given a Professorship by Lord Abergavenny at the College of Burgh Apton. He held his appointment for fifteen years, resigning in 1852. Two years later, at Marylebone, he passed away.

Professor Jenkinson was an amazing personality. He began to lecture to the Inner Circle on many subjects. They embraced not only the spirit world, but he discussed many problems that face us in our everyday life on this earth. But the most amazing gift he brought down to the medium at that time was that of painting. While on earth, he had been a great art lover, and his lifelong hobby was painting.

A short time after he came to their meetings he produced, through the hand of the medium, the first painting—without paints! He materialised the colours he required through the tips of Walsh's fingers! He would draw the outline of the subject on paper with a pencil or fountain pen.

Then he would shake the fingers of the medium over the outline, and the coloured paints required would pass through the tips of the fingers and appear on the paper exactly where required. The first experiments in this direction were rather crude, but as he was able to develop this gift more efficiently through the instrument, so the quality of the paintings improved also.

7

THE INNER CIRCLE

Friends show me what I can do

SCHILLER

At this stage it might be advisable to give brief descriptions of the personalities that comprised the closed Tuesday night Inner Circle. The reason being that I shall soon be describing the amazing gifts of materialisation, spirit painting and luminosity that developed in the above circle—gifts that were so unusual that many may find it hard to believe that these events really happened. These strange gifts could only be developed in the presence of people who had wonderful faith and implicit belief in what they witnessed and heard from the guides through Walsh.

The guides called this Inner Circle the 'Temple of God' and each of the chosen followers was called a 'pillar' of the Temple. The first pillar was Stan Walsh. I did not attempt to whitewash his faults in the early chapters, so now I want to record some more of his virtues.

To his family he was a wonderful son and brother. Being single he lived at home with his ageing parents and their daughter, Norma, who also never married. I would sometimes visit him on weekends, stroll through the back gate, tap at the back door and walk in. Sometimes I would find Stan doing odd jobs in the house for his parents, or pottering about in his tiny garden, which he used to pet and stroke with loving care. At one time, when his father was seriously ill, he nursed him as tenderly as a woman.

His father continually called for Stan in his delirium and he would sit up all night attending his sick parent.

His brother, Cecil, who had passed on some time earlier was often there giving advice to Stan clairaudiently, warning him of little family problems or worries and how to avoid or overcome them. The family did not realise that it was his psychic gifts that enabled him to advise or help them so accurately.

On one occasion his mother said to me, 'Stan has an extraordinary knack of saying the right thing at the right time. He seems to sense what is going to happen beforehand, and we have learnt to take his advice, because he is always right'.

He often called upon his psychic gifts to help strangers in distress at unexpected times and in unexpected places. Two instances stand out from the many. On one occasion he was walking along the beach at Middle Park. Being tired he sat down on a seat nearby. A middle aged woman sat on the same seat. Somehow he felt she was in trouble. He was drawn to talk to her. He began to talk about her past life; he then went on to tell what was troubling her, to which she listened open mouthed. Then the guide—it was the spirit of Angus Du Font impressing his mind—told her that she would get complete relief from her trouble, and much sooner than she realised.

When he got up to go, she said to him, 'I don't know how to thank you.

I feel as if a great weight has been lifted off my mind. But—how do you know all about me? I don't know you!' 'Oh, I just know', smiled Stan, and walked rapidly away.

On another occasion he was at the cemetery tidying up his brother, Cecils' grave. He noticed a woman at a nearby grave which had obviously just been filled in. She seemed to be in great distress. Then he saw the spirit of a young man close to her, with his hand on her shoulder; so he walked over and said, 'Excuse me, but you know you should not be so upset. I can see the spirit of your son, whose name is Arthur, standing next to you trying to console you. He asks me to tell you that he is quite all right now, and will come close to you many times and guide you through life.' Then he went on to describe her son to the amazed woman including what he looked like and how he was killed through a motor bike accident.

'Thank you so much', she said, 'I don't know who you are, but you described my son perfectly. You have given me great comfort.' It was the practice in those days at Christmas time for shops in suburbs to place a large bottle in the window full of peas or beans. Shoppers had to guess how many were in the bottle. The prize for the winner was a large Christmas stocking. One year Stan put in several guesses at a local shop which his family patronised. And he won! He walked out of the shop triumphantly and invited me to go along with him to a family in Dorcas St, South Melbourne where there were five children. The father was out of work, for this was during the depression, and the family could hardly scrape enough money for food, so the prospects of a Merry Christmas for the children was bleak. When Stan knocked at the door and presented the huge stocking to the mother and children, the shrieks of delight from the children were worth going a long way to hear.

This was the man, Walsh. He was always thinking of others—never of himself. There was nothing false or artificial about him. He was always just himself. It was his utter guilelessness which made any suggestion of deceit or trickery on his part so impossible. This helped to convince others.

The second Pillar was Bert Jones, sometimes called Herb or Herby Jones or even Jonesy. He was Stan's closest friend for twenty years. Hundreds of housewives in the Newmarket district knew him for many years as 'Baker'.

He was highly respected and very popular with all clients on his bread-carting round. Many a time when one of these families were short of cash and could not pay for a loaf, Bert obliged out of his own pocket. He was cautious, very careful and shrewd. He was a power of strength to Stan and possessed something which Stan lacked—a firmness in the face of caressing coercion, which could not be melted. Stan could never say 'No' to anyone who pleaded with him, often in pathetic tones, for a message from the guides. But Bert could say 'No' with the greatest of ease, and often said it very bluntly to silly or persistent men or women who had no regard for Walsh's health, as long as they got a message.

He was abrupt, and often very stubborn, yet at heart he had a real softness and sentimentality. Sometimes his temper flared up and he would give vent to an abrupt barrage of blunt words which cleared the air and helped to quickly disperse undesirable elements which tried to impose on Stan's good natured and easy going ways.

He was a classic example of a 'rough diamond'. Looking back upon my old friend I would say that he was like the proverbial dog that shows its teeth at one end, wags his tail at the other. Undoubtedly he always finished up by praying for all and sundry—even for those he had growled at.

That was Bert! Mrs Martin was the Third Pillar. She was the hostess of the Inner Circle and a typical Australian mother. She was a widow with four children whom she had reared by herself to adulthood. Sound, astute and practical, she was a keen political student and an avid reader of good books. One would have difficulty in deceiving her. Twenty years of battling with tradesmen, lodgers and all types of humanity on her own, as well as being both mother and father to four lusty, energetic children, had enabled her to develop a gift of sizing up the characters of anyone she met with unerring accuracy.

To her Stan Walsh was the soul of goodness. She confided to me at one time that his child-like simplicity, his guilelessness and transparent honesty were qualities that convinced her of the truths enunciated through him—far more so than the actual phenomena itself. 'Such a man is utterly incapable of deceit, even if it were possible to do so,' she concluded.

The fourth pillar was Mabel Grenville. A lifelong single woman and a schoolteacher for over forty years, and a Bachelor of Arts, Mabel was thin and tall with straight black hair drawn firmly back from a well developed forehead. She had rather a small face housing a pair of beautiful dark brown eyes which seemed to emit sparks of fire when she was excited.

She was a brilliant Bible student, and was as familiar with her Bible as a postman is with his postal round. Mabel's cover was nothing like the book within. Inside was a typical Australian country woman. All her family were pioneers and she used to astonish her hearers with the apt way she gave expression, at times, to Australian colloquialisms, such as 'Fair Dinkum', 'Bonzer Bloke', 'Over the Fence' and so on, all mixed up with learned dissertations on various subjects she might be discussing. This grim looking woman had a very keen sense of humour and a 'heart as soft as butter' as Bert described her. She was a secret good Samaritan, forever climbing in and out of trams and buses with large, mysterious bags full of good things for all types of people in needy circumstances.

These were the four Pillars of the Inner Circle. Four strong and original characters with more than their fair share of common sense and a wonderful, child-like faith in God—truly faithful, sensible persons.

8

UNPROGRESSED SPIRITS

> When my brother sins against me, how often should I forgive him? Seven times?
>
> PETER THE APOSTLE

After some months the Inner Circle began to spread its wings. Another weekly meeting was arranged, this time on Thursdays, at the Thornbury home of Mrs Martin's married brother, Viv Matherson. Later, at the continual requests from friends, Sunday afternoon meetings were started. Sunday night meetings were kept for interested outsiders, at Mrs Martin's home; admission was by invitation only.

A year or so later Walsh and Jones were invited to other homes, usually on Saturday night. The weekly Tuesday meeting of the Inner Circle, however, remained closed to new members for many years. Finally one more member was admitted in 1927—myself. It was at these little gatherings that all new gifts were developed.

Shortly after the Thursday meetings started, Viv Matherson expressed his fear of 'evil spirits'. The next Thursday Angus Du Font came and lectured to them on this subject. Miss Grenville took some notes and handed them to me later.

The gist of his remarks was this: You must not call them 'evil spirits'. No spirit in the sight of God is altogether 'evil'. They are 'unprogressed spirits'. Many of these are drawn towards séances. They are lonely, in darkness, often resentful; usually they long for the company of human beings, and need help. We shall be bringing many of them to all your meetings from time to time in an endeavour to bring happiness into their lives.

Be sure, therefore, not to drive them away when we allow them to speak through the instrument, try and make friends with them. Speak to them kindly and send your loving thoughts towards them. All spirits, no matter how low they may have fallen, are the children of God. One day they must all eventually rise again and go back to the great heart of God from whence they originally came.

The lower planes of darkness are full of potential prodigal sons and daughters. Each one will, some day, 'come to himself or herself, and want to go back home—when that time comes, spiritual helpers, in the name of God, will 'run to meet them'. You should do likewise. If they sincerely want to better themselves, they need human encouragement—and YOU can give it.

Faithful and dedicated people of every religion, concentrate on saving souls on earth, but it is just as important that every lost or wayward man or woman who passes out of the physical body and goes to the darkened or lower planes of the spirit world should also be saved. The orthodox opinion prevalent in many religions is that once a person has sinned greatly and dies unrepentant, his chance of salvation has gone. That is not true. No one is ever lost forever. The lowest of the low will eventually be saved by God.

There are no hell fires! Everyone who commits evil on earth makes his own hell or purgatory. When these souls pass out of the physical body they dwell in a darkness created by themselves, a darkness brought about by sinful acts and thoughts. Not only do they make their own 'hell', but the 'Wrath of God' which earlier generations heard so much about is, in fact, the wrath of their own soul.

The soul within us all, is a spark of God—or whatever we may prefer to call the deific universal force that pervades all. It is absolutely indestructible. It is the immortal spark deep down within, which rebukes a sinner who has passed into the world of spirit.

When those who are lost first try to find their way home again, no angel in heaven is too high to come down and help that repenting soul, whether they are still on the earth plane or over here in spirit, they are never 'lost'.

Jesus, Himself, continually comes down to the darkened planes to help those who are temporarily lost, or who are in utter despair. He speaks to these self imprisoned souls many times. Actually these remarks of Du Font's are verified in the New Testament in 1st Peter, Chapter 3, Verse 19.

Their prison is of their own making and they remain there until they, themselves, turn towards God. One day they will do so. They may roam close to the earth for years, earthbound and in darkness, but eventually someone's prayers or loving thoughts, which are the same thing, coming up from the earth plane, or down from the spiritual planes of light, will bring comfort and understanding into their unhappy souls. The realisation that God loves them, and will continue to do so for all eternity gradually brings the desire to better themselves. Once they allow themselves to be touched by the saving grace of God's love, these lost souls gradually find their way back to their Inheritance.

You can understand, therefore, why your sincere love, friendship and prayers can do much in that direction. Many of these 'unprogressed' or 'weak spirits' have died in the slums, or in prison, or through violence, murder, execution, or self abuse. In many cases it seemed that every man's hand had been against them. Many have lost all hope. They are crushed by sin and are in utter despair. It is wrong, therefore, to drive them away when they sorely need your help.

You may ask: Why is it so important that we in the flesh should help these unhappy ones? The answer is: When on the earth plane they are often condemned by human beings. But if they wander into your homes and find that there are some human beings who do not condemn them, but, instead, love them, that is, want to help them, that makes all the difference.

You might also think: If the angels in heaven are eager to help them, why can't they prevail in such cases? The explanation is: Thoughts of love and kindness coming towards these less progressed spirits from frail human minds can do more for them than all the angels' prayers, because they don't understand angels yet. Understanding of higher spiritual beings will come later. They only understand human beings in the flesh. Encouraged by human beings, these souls can then be helped by high spiritual guides, or angels if you like. When you ask God to take spiritual strength from your soul, in love, to help these poor souls you give your guides an opportunity to say to them: 'If ordinary human beings like this love you and pray for you—how much more must God love you? How much more must Jesus love you?' These are logical questions that these lost children of God cannot gainsay.

The first thing these weak spirits are taught is that they will begin to find peace within themselves as soon as they realise that they must wipe out the evil, or undo the harm, that they committed on earth. They begin to understand that they cannot find true happiness until they make total reparation. For instance: if a person has been responsible, while on earth, for leading many astray, or bringing hardship or suffering into the lives of others, he must try in the spirit world to undo the wrong he has created. Sins of commission or omission can only be wiped out by atonement— that is, by bringing those whom they have wronged back to the path of happiness. This they can do by trying to influence for good the minds they have injured; or by fighting hard to guide these minds towards happiness or success.

On earth, a man may have destroyed many by his greed or rapacity, or by evilly influencing the lives of others; he was, in short, a 'destroying anger. But, now in spirit, after arduous progression, this same repentant spirit could come again into the lives of those he had harmed on earth as a Guardian Angel! Only in this way do the converted persons in spirit wipe out their sins, and commence their journey back to God in peace.

These remarks by Angus Du Font on expiation in the spirit world, can be understood if we relate them to what is being attempted on the earth plane. Suggestions have been made in the papers from time to time that all reckless motorists who kill or maim people on the roads should be made to work in hospitals if possible as wardsmen where their maimed victims lie so that they may help to restore these to health. If their victims are killed, they should be made to offer some monetary or other recompense to the next of kin, and so wipe out the debt. Again: it has been suggested in various papers that vandals who destroy or deface public utilities be made to repair or clean these damaged or mutilated places themselves.

When I attended the meetings I learnt of many instances where this form of expiation, explained so clearly by Du Font, was practised in the spirit world. Here is one example, one of many: During the late twenties and early thirties a notorious Melbourne criminal, Squizzy Taylor, who had often made newspaper headlines, was shot dead in a gunfight. He came back in spirit some time later, in great distress, asking us to help him. We did so, and encouraged him as much as we could. As time went on he returned, a very happy spirit. He said that he had risen to a higher plane. He had achieved this by helping others, and that, he said, was his work now.

We asked him the nature of that work. He said: 'I come down and mingle with the people I know on earth. I find them in criminal quarters, in gaols and all sorts of strange places. I try to influence their minds and prevent them from committing crimes they are planning. Often I am successful, although not always, of course. But if I am, I find that, knowing how they think, I can get into their minds and bring the understanding to them that they lack. Through progression and constant study over here I have acquired a "new language", and if I were to try and impress their minds as I think and understand now, they would ignore my thoughts. I must think in their language, not the language I have since learnt. To explain a little more, if I were to try and impress their minds according to my present way of thinking, by saying: "What you contemplate doing is evil in the sight of God" it would not register with them other than as a silly thought. But if I forcibly place a thought in their mind, such as: "Listen, mate. If you break into that joint, you'll cop the lot. Dice it. It's a mug's game." THAT thought registers. It might make him hesitate, through fear, or it might be taken as a premonition, and he gives up the idea. From then onward I keep working on his mind until I can induce him to turn to an honest living. It's hard work and I don't always succeed. But even though success is rare I find, when it does come, it gives me a wonderful feeling of exhilaration—I know that I am progressing spiritually as I help others to progress. That's why I need YOUR constant prayers as they give ME greater strength to succeed.'

Many other well known criminals and evil doers who have passed on, came through the trance mediumship of Walsh. Help was readily given to them all by the members of these circles, and the same thing happened to all these lost souls. They were encouraged by the love and friendship of Walsh and his followers to make atonement by saving others, and so earn forgiveness. I have heard and spoken to many of these unhappy ones— eventually, all, through the help of members of these meetings and of the guides, were sent on along the road of progression and happiness.

One night, after the guides had been explaining how the very lowest must one day return to God as angels, Mrs Martin, who was a very thorough, down-to-earth person, said, at supper time: 'You know, I can't help thinking. If any person, no matter how low they fall, or what evil they commit on earth, must eventually become an angel of God, what sense is there in trying to be good? Why not eat, drink and be merry all your life. You'll still finish up in heaven!' A heated discussion took place, then, suddenly, Professor Jenkinson took control of Stan and said: 'My friends. Do not forget that a person who leads an evil life, suffers in proportion to the sins he or she has committed—often in darkness and despair and anguish for many years. If you sin you must pay the price. If a person on earth deliberately leads a selfish and evil life they do not realise what terrible punishment, as I have just mentioned, awaits them even if it is a punishment self inflicted. Also, do not forget that one aspect of God is justice. We are 'judged' not only by the life we live, but this judgment also takes into consideration the particular environment in which we have lived, and not how it affected our every-day behaviour.

Children of criminal, vicious or bad living parents are set a bad example by these elders and grow up not knowing any better. There are all sorts of unhappy and evil conditions that affect an immature mind brought up in bad homes. These are not known to man, but seen and understood by God. Is it possible that God, who is LOVE, could condemn a soul to everlasting damnation?'

9

A BLUEPRINT FOR ETERNITY

In deep waters men find great pearls

PROVERB

Du Font and Jenkinson, together with other guides, constantly impressed upon the members of the Inner Circle the importance of earnest prayer, for the medium, for each other and for the continued development of the spiritual power of the Circle.

They were urged to seek and pray for:

Only the best and highest spiritual gifts.

For God's will to control and govern every activity in their circle, and to give power to the guides in everything they did. (No Guide had power, they said, to accomplish anything unless given strength by God.)

To regard their séances as sacred. To approach the meetings in the same spirit as they would enter a church.

Not to call themselves 'Spiritualists'—simply 'Followers of the Truth of God'.

Not to allow anyone to come to any of the séances on any night without express permission of the guides—and no visitors, whatsoever to the Inner Circle on Tuesday night.

To wear a simple white robe at all meetings. The type required was a loose, easy fitting gown which one could put on over one's every-day wear. The gowns, they said, were the symbolic expression of the putting off of all material thoughts which could in any way mar the spiritual atmosphere of the meetings.

To pray and help all weak spirits brought into the room by the guides for encouragement and help.

Actually Walsh and his followers were being asked to dedicate themselves completely to their spiritual work. This is what they did as the years went on. It was the secret of the extraordinary gifts that were unceasingly given to Walsh. The earnestness and devotion in obeying, as far as humanly possible, the precepts of the guides led to astonishing results.

The first noticeable result was that guides from higher and yet higher planes began to come down and speak through the instrument. Guides such as Vashti, an Egyptian Priest who lived 4000 years ago, Armah Singh, a Hindu seer who lived in the fifteenth century, Joan of Arc, the French Saint and St Teresa of Lisieux (The Little Flower).

Then came guides from the highest plane of all—the eleventh spiritual plane—Biblical personalities included Abraham the Jewish patriarch, Samuel the Prophet, King David, Ruth and Naomi (the latter, Naomi, came to me as a guide, a year or so after I joined their circle). Many of Christ's disciples and followers visited us—Mary Magdalene, John the Baptist, Matthew, Peter, Mark, John, the most beloved, Paul, Stephen the first Martyr and many others.

Many who read this may, perhaps smile. That would be natural. When outsiders heard of these high visitations they said: 'Even if it were true, why should this insignificant man, a mere carpenter in a small factory, be chosen as an instrument to be used by these exalted beings from the highest planes?' To answer these we found it useful to draw attention to remarks made by the orthodox priests of Christ's day: 'Why should this man, a common carpenter, be chosen as the Messiah.' Walsh was chosen as a prophet of modern times, and when these lofty souls spoke through him his followers were convinced beyond all doubt— more so, as they emphasised their presence by bringing with them amazing new powers.

After hearing them speak, we who heard them, could only repeat what the soldiers said to the High Priests about Jesus: 'Never man spake like this man!' I remember a local school teacher who came to many of the Sunday night meetings. He had known Walsh for almost a lifetime. He said, 'It is incredible that such beautiful language and deep wisdom could flow from the lips of an untaught man, such as Walsh.' At this stage it is fitting to mention a small incident which happened to Walsh when these high guides first started to visit the Inner Circle. When they brought with them new spiritual gifts, he began to wonder if he would ever travel and spread the Truth they were enunciating to people in other lands. He did not directly seek this information but, being only human, he pondered about it a lot.

Often as he worked at his saw bench in the factory, his thoughts turned to this subject; so much so that he began to be discontented with his lot.

Why should he be bound to a bench covered with saw dust, hammering and working away at a monotonous wood-work job when he could be doing wonderful things in other parts of the world? Then one day he had just run a big piece of timber through the buzz-saw when he was suddenly shown a vision. He found himself looking into another carpenter's room, and at another carpenter's bench. At that bench, quietly sawing wood with an old fashioned Jewish saw was a man— Jesus of Nazareth. The vision faded, but the meaning was obvious. He had learnt his lesson. Never again was he to be discontented with his job.

We assumed it coincidence that Walsh, like the Master he in later life chose to serve under so selflessly, also worked for his living as a carpenter.

This was the only hint given that there was any 'plan' in this, but no doubt the knowledge must have often comforted Walsh.

10

AN AWAKENING

One door shuts, but another opens

IRISH PROVERB

To explain my personal involvement with this story I must relate some of the events that occurred in my life just prior to my first meeting with Walsh. For years I was a book keeper in an office of a merchandising company in Fitzroy. My leisure time was devoted to a favourite hobby, ventriloquism. I became an amateur entertainer in this field. Practice and experience gave me a professional touch, so by the age of twenty I was giving paid performances at all kinds of night shows.

When I reached twenty-two years I longed to travel around Australia, so I gave up my daytime work and became a full time professional ventriloquist. This was in 1922. After many tours around Australia, and appearances in Melbourne and Sydney in silent picture shows, I came back to Melbourne in 1924.

I was in need of further material for my act, and sought out a scriptwriter who had been recommended to me. He lived in Bridge Road, Richmond and there I met his daughter, Winnie. She was a young widow with a small son, from her first marriage, named Ron. An immediate friendship sprang up.

Winnie and I were married in 1925. We had only been married a year when she died giving birth to our first child. This unborn baby girl died with her.

This was my first experience of death in my own family and I was shattered. I felt as if some unseen hand had taken hold of Winnie, thrust her into the dark chamber of death and slammed the door in my face. It was as if life had lost all meaning. It was cruel and ruthless. At this tragic period of my life I was an atheist. I had no belief in anything that I could not see or hear or touch.

Several days after the burial I went alone to the St Kilda cemetery to look at Winnie's grave. I stood there despondently wondering what sort of tombstone and kerbing I should have erected. There was such a desperate feeling of finality about this last decision for my wife. Considering my refusal to accept any spiritual concepts, what I experienced next was inexplicable! Suddenly I heard, inwardly—but clear and unmistakable — the voice of my wife say: 'Don't spend too much on the grave, dear—I'm not there'.

I was startled, and looked around. There was not a soul near me. I could not understand how it came about. Finally I put it down to my imagination, but I was never really satisfied. The voice had been so clear and distinct, so unexpected. Later I found myself thinking about it often and wondering. It was not until I later met Stan Walsh that I understood that what I had experienced was my introduction to the gift known as 'clairaudience'.

I left the cemetery that day and decided to try and forget the past by plunging again into interminable touring around Australia. I left my stepson, Ron, again with Winnie's mother. My outlook on life was cynical.

After a long tour of Queensland towns, I eventually arrived back in Brisbane. There I met, unexpectedly, an old vaudeville friend who was a member of a comedy team known as Ward and Sherman. Sherman was a Jewish intellectual. He had a much more serious mind and ability to exercise it than the usual vaudeville folk of those days. He confided in me that he had developed the art of automatic writing.

This was my introduction to the subject. I later came to realize that is one of the oldest known, and most commonly used, forms of communication from the world of spirit.

I subsequently learnt that every religion has its inspired writings which are nothing more or less than messages dictated to, and transcribed by, earth mediums. In many cases they are acknowledged cases of automatic writing where the medium did not really understand what he was writing.

The Bible is the most classic example of automatic and inspired writing. Few would dispute its inspirational aspect and fewer still the Divine motives for using certain scribes in this way.

Another classic example of a massive written work which is claimed to have been 'dictated' from spirit sources is the Oahspe which came into existence in the year 1881 through the mediumship of Dr John Ballou Newborough, a noted medical doctor and psychical researcher. He became impatient with the slowness of reception and the lowliness of much of the spiritual message being received through conventional mediumistic means. He prescribed for himself a course involving diet and other purifying methods whereby his body would become sufficiently pure to invite the communication of very high spirits. In this way he hoped to be instrumental in the reception of spiritual knowledge of a higher calibre. He included in his preparation the acquisition, and learning to manipulate, of one of the newly invented writing machines known as a 'typewriter'. It was directly onto this machine that he finally wrote, in one year and without really knowing what he was writing, one of the most vast and amazing works in history. It is believed to contain the sacred history of this earth under the dominion of God and His spiritual co-workers on the various heavenly planes. This complex history includes a synopsis of the whole cosmic Universe and its purpose was to give man an increase in knowledge to equip him to face the information explosion of the twentieth century and to re-affirm God's supreme, Deific Presence.

Many of history's greatest poets and authors have claimed that their writing was inspired or 'not their own'. Holy men of all the great religions including the Saints of the Christian Church have given repeated credit for their writings and records to 'higher sources', 'divine guidance' or 'spiritual inspiration'.

Had I known or given serious thought to this subject before that reunion with Sherman, I would have been better prepared for the events to follow.

Coming back to my friend, Sherman, I asked him what he meant by automatic writing? He explained, 'A spirit force takes hold of my right hand, and I find it, without any effort on my part, being propelled across the paper. When the hand is still, there is a message in bold, round handwriting from the spirit world, either for me or someone else'.

Several days after Sherman had told me about his power, we were sitting in his flat talking, when suddenly he felt impelled to pick up a pencil and writing pad from his desk. When he sat down his right hand began to write furiously across the paper. When it stopped he picked up the pad, read it, and then handed the pad to me. The words written were: 'Tell Les I will speak to him soon—Win'.

I was surprised, but doubtful. After all, he knew my wife's name was Win, and it was quite possible that he might have been driven, unwittingly, to write the words by his subconscious mind. And yet—why give such an impossible message?

How could I speak to her, or she to me? After all, he could just as easily have written: Tell Les I am alive', or some such message, which could not be proved or disproved.

So I said to him, 'How on earth can Win speak to me?' He laughed and replied, 'Don't ask me. I have nothing to do with it. Why not wait and see?'

Several months later I found myself back again in Melbourne, and it was then that this promise given through the hand of my friend was kept.

Certain theatrical friends told me of a wonderful deep-trance medium in Albert Park. He was called Stan Walsh. I was by now puzzled and curious enough to be interested. My friends were able to induce Walsh to let me come along to one of his Sunday night meetings.

On the night I arrived I was introduced to a room full of strangers, and then told, 'This is Mr Walsh'. I found myself shaking hands with a small, slightly built man with large, dark brown eyes, brilliant and penetrating. When he smiled his eyes seemed to light up the whole of his face.

Then the séance began; a hymn was sung, a prayer was given and then followed a lecture by a spirit guide called Vashti. I noted at the time that I was astonished by what he said of the afterlife. Later several other spirit visitors spoke to sundry members or sitters, either through the direct voice trumpet, or through the medium.

This went on for about an hour, and then, a woman's voice was heard coming from the lips of the medium under deep-trance. She called me by name, and when I answered she said it was 'Win'! She spoke to me, and I to her. It was an eager, emotionally charged conversation in which she talked to me of many intimate incidents in our past life, of her care and guidance for Ron, her son by her first marriage, and many other personal matters known only to ourselves.

AN AWAKENING

I was convinced beyond all doubt. I left this house of strangers with my head in a whirl. Life, it seemed, did have some meaning. The dull, grey cloud of loneliness and desolation that had enveloped me for more than a year, since Win died, seemed to have lifted. As I walked, or should I say 'floated', home, I recalled the message given to me by my Jewish friend some months before. Tell Les that I will speak to him soon—Win.' SHE DID!

At home, late that night, I sat deep in thought. I realised that the unseen hand that had slammed the door on my happy-go-lucky past life with Win, was the hand of God. But I also realised that the revelation that had come to me that night, that there was no death, was also from God.

He had opened another door to me; a door that was to lead to great changes in my life, and much happiness.

11

THE CHALLENGE

> A bore is a person who insists on talking about himself,
> when you want to talk about yourself
>
> GEORGE BERNARD SHAW

The effect of that unusual Sunday episode convinced me of the certainty of Eternity - like a soft, cool wind it had blown out of my heart the dreary grey mists that had enveloped it during the last year since I lost my wife. I was born again. But although my head was up among the stars, I kept my feet firmly on the ground.

I was invited to attend regularly every Sunday night, but I had to think of my future. I earned my living in the theatre, and in free-lance writing for periodicals and journals. The theatre kept me away from Melbourne most of the time, so I began to plan ahead.

I was never really happy in show business; it was too uncertain. So I started to look for another job—a daytime job. I secured a position as assistant to the accountant of a shoe factory in Collingwood. Now I could attend the Sunday meetings. I began to form a warm and deep friendship with Walsh and the Inner Circle members. Soon I was invited to come also to the Thursday meetings.

One Sunday night a few months later, after I had settled down to my day position, I was told by Malocca that I had been chosen by the guides to join the Inner circle on Tuesday nights. I was quite surprised and elated. Strangely, my ever increasing psychic involvements did not affect my material commitments. In fact, the spiritual experiences, on the nights already mentioned, acted as a decided stimulus to my daily responsibilities.

The Company began to grow, and I grew with it. As the months went by it opened up branch factories in three outlying suburbs. Then their accountant retired and I was promoted to the job left vacant. I was appointed, not only as accountant, but also as secretary of the company, with a much bigger staff to control than when I first started.

My life had now taken on a definite pattern—a hard, but challenging job during the day, and three nights a week communing with the saints and near saints! I loved the ebb and flow of these continual material and spiritual activities.

My reference to these personal episodes in my own life may seem on the surface, irrelevant to the essential message of this book but I include them, nevertheless, because they show that I was a definite eye witness to all that happened during the last twelve, and most important, years of Walsh's mission on earth. In this they ARE relevant.

It also gives me the authority to explain each of Stan's gifts. Apart from the minor gifts of Automatic Writing, Clairvoyance and Clairaudience— there were those of Deep-trance; Materialisation, or Apports; Materialised Painting; Direct Voice—amplified through trumpet and Luminosity, or Transfiguration.

I became a member of these meetings when the first four gifts had already developed. But the luminosity, and manifestations of light, did not develop until after I had been drawn into the Inner Circle. It was a gift that developed slowly and only within the above circle. When it reached its peak, however, which was about a year after I had joined, the guides said it would then be shown to outsiders—that is, at the Thursday and Sunday night meetings when strangers were admitted.

By this time I was well established in business, and I was also completely converted to the Christian faith. My instruction in Christian faith came from the guides and was truly ecumenical in spirit and above sectarianism. As a result I have been able to feel at home in any Christian Church and at complete ease and peace with all fellow Christians—and indeed all men of any belief or non-belief. In later years I became a member of the Presbyterian Church, but it has been said to me by Catholics that I understand more about the Catholic faith than most Catholics, and I have been able to take my place as a Lay Preacher in all pulpits of other faiths.

Such is the Spirit of God, that men can come together in love and confidence, from all walks of life and all creeds, to worship, pray and study as one body. As a member of the Inner Circle, I became not only a 'follower of the Truth of God' and aware of the certainty of Eternity, but I also discovered the full meaning of Christ's instruction that we must 'love one another'.

12

THEY WERE ALL AMAZED

The Law of Truth was in his mouth

MALACHI: 2-6

Deep-trance mediumship, according to Professor Jenkinson, is a rare phenomenon. There are many imitators, but very few genuine ones. Deep-trance, he said, was similar to that received by the followers of Christ on the day of Pentecost. On that day this gift was showered with profusion upon many, which was understandable. They were forerunners or message bearers of the Christian religion, and they were sent out with this deep-trance gift to every country in the known world of that day.

Jenkinson's reference to Pentecost relates to the phenomena recorded in the Bible in the Book of Acts. It says: 'they were all filled with the Holy Ghost and began to speak with other tongues...and the multitude were confounded, because every man heard them speak in his own language. And they were all amazed and marvelled, saying, 'Behold, are not all these that speak Galileans? And how hear we every man in our own tongue wherein we were born?'

And so it was with Walsh. Spirits of different nationalities; German, French, Italian, Hindustani, and so on, all spoke to their friends or relatives on earth, in their own tongue, through Walsh's mediumship.

One of his early followers and staunchest friends was a large, imposing Jewish lady called Mrs Langley. She had the manners of a duchess, a voice like Lady MacBeth and heart of gold. For years she had special meetings once a month at the flats, where she lived at St Kilda. She used to discuss family and private problems with her late husband's spirit, in Hebrew. She conversed with some of her other friends who came through, in Yiddish.

Another follower was a young Greek called Angie Gurdes. His father often spoke to him through Walsh in the Greek language. I listened to a French woman talk to her mother, in spirit, in the French tongue; an Italian speak to his spirit brother in Italian; a German soldier came through and spoke in German to an Australian Major, who could speak German fluently.

Is it any wonder, then, that many of the eye witnesses at these meetings should use similar terms to that said at Pentecost: 'How is it that this man, an Australian, with a very limited education, can talk to anyone of any nationality in the latter's own tongue fluently?'

And many an educated man who came to these meetings remarked: 'How can this unlettered man, under trance, give learned discussions on all sorts of abstruse subjects in a cultured voice, perfectly expressed, without one grammatical error?' The answer to these and similar questions is: Because under deep trance, any person can come back and control both body and mind of the medium, and enable that spirit person to reveal himself exactly as he was on earth, learned or unlearned, and with the exact type of personality peculiar to him when on earth.

It was these features about Walsh's deep-trance powers that convinced and impressed so many.

One of the strange aspects of deep trance is that when a spirit comes back for the first time, he or she reverts to the physical condition which they were in immediately prior to death. If they died in agony, they came back in agony; if they died short of breath they came back with the same condition; if a person left the body suffering from a throat disease, he or she would come back choking and gasping for breath. All the symptoms of pain and distress were given to the medium.

One of the tasks assigned to Jones by the guides was to assist spirits, who came through for the first time, to throw off these painful conditions.

Jones would massage the medium's body. In the foregoing example he would speak encouragingly to the spirit and then proceed to massage the medium's throat. Magnetism would flow from Jones' hands and gradually clear away this painful condition.

The guides explained that this is natural for a spirit when it contacts flesh and blood again, to recall exactly how he or she felt just before death. Massaging by Jones helped to remove these distressing conditions, and no further last minute sufferings would occur with any subsequent control of the medium by the same spirit.

Genuine deep-trance has to be seen to be fully appreciated. It is NOT something that can be developed, acquired or learnt. It is a gift of God given to whom He wills, and when He wills. Very few born into this world are able, or fit, to bear the peculiar strain it entails.

Someone once asked Malocca why Walsh was chosen to be a deep-trance medium. His reply was simple and to the point. He said it was 'because of his purity of thought'. This reply speaks volumes. It also explains why those from the very highest planes—the High Guides—were able to speak through him. I read recently where Queen Elizabeth visited certain humble homes of ordinary working people. The report said that 'each housewife in the homes selected, made sure that her abode was clean and spotless'. In the same way the highest in the spirit world can only enter the fleshly temple of those whose minds are clean and pure. Absolute purity cannot dwell in impure surroundings.

It was a never ending wonder to see this quietly spoken, simple mannered man taken over by some powerful personality from the spirit world. Perhaps a Red Indian Chief with a deep, harsh, almost bellowing voice, oozing power and dynamic magnetism. Although Walsh was just a little over five feet tall, he appeared on such occasions, in illusion of course, to be well over six feet. It was understandable for a guide to explain that the Indian Chief in question was, on earth, nearly seven feet tall.

Professor Jenkinson once lectured on deep-trance. He explained that a strong spiritual guide is sent down by God to stand by the trance medium. This guide is what is called the Spiritual Doorkeeper. Other terms used are 'Guide of that person's life'. The Catholic religion teaches that each one of us has a Guardian Angel, which is correct, and is exactly the same spiritual entity mentioned above.

In the above case the chief guide or guardian angel of Stan Walsh was Malocca. It was his responsibility to see that only those spirits, whom God wills, take control of the body. Malocca stood at the door of the medium's mind, as it were, and barred the way to any but those whom he knows he could safely allow to control the instrument. At the beginning of a séance, the doorkeeper, Malocca, always came through first, to 'open the door' of the medium's mind. When the séance was finished, he always came back to clear any conditions from the mind of the medium which might worry him. Malocca would then 'shut the door'.

The transfer, or exchange of souls, or spirits, at the point of control must be made in a split second. The soul of the medium suddenly moves out, and to the side, of the body, but still connected to it by a thin, invisible ethereal 'cord'. This 'cord' is referred to in Ecclesiastes, Chapter 12: Verses 5 and 6, where reference is made to man's death, and the 'silver cord' is loosed, or broken.

As the soul of the medium swiftly moves out, the doorkeeper or spirit about to control the body, moves in. It then completely controls the brain, nervous system and all the other bodily functions operating within the human instrument. In other words—control of the body completely changes hands.

This swift change could be likened to one motor driver getting out of his car and letting another driver take his place. The latter might be just as experienced as the first in driving, but if he has not driven this particular car he has taken over, it might take him just a little while to get used to the gears and general 'feel' of this strange car.

So it is with a spirit from the spirit world entering the body of the medium. Sometimes it takes just a little while to get used to the strange body he is using. The spirit was used to controlling a body on earth, but not this one. This 'strangeness' may at first lead to a certain amount of gasping or stuttering, or a few slight bodily or facial contortions before the new driver settles in and can be himself—or somebody else's self!

Again, of course, it often happens that a spirit is too weak, that is, one that has come from a low plane in the spirit world, to control the body. So the doorkeeper controls the instrument, with the exception of the throat, the voice box and mouth muscles. The weak one is then encouraged to try and use this throat and mouth. In such cases articulation is, at first, slow and very faint, but as the spirit gains confidence he finds that he is able to speak quite clearly.

If by chance the 'silver cord' were to break while the body was being occupied by another spirit, death of the medium would take place immediately. This, however, does not happen, because the doorkeeper, or chief guide, is a very high spirit and has shown, beyond all doubt, his ability to guard and completely protect and control the medium under any circumstances. Briefly, whoever happens to control the body at the time does so by the express will of God, as expressed through the chosen doorkeeper.

While someone was speaking through the medium, the disembodied soul or spirit of Walsh was held by another spirit guide close to the physical body. Also, as the conscious mind is occupied by an outside spirit entity, it is obvious that when the original 'owner' of the body returns to take control, he is quite unconscious of what has been going on, because his mind and brain have been used by someone else.

There were occasions, however, when the disembodied soul of Walsh was able to remember for a few fleeting moments what was going on while he was out of his body. He spoke of the uncanny feeling of looking down on himself from a few feet above, and watching it walk about, speaking, some times in a strange tongue to those in the room. Also the weird feeling of looking at his human face strangely altered by the spirit controlling it.

But these occasions were rare. Mostly what he recalled, when in the spirit world, was what he saw when he was lifted up to high planes of light. When the spirit forces finished using the body the same lightning flash change took place. Walsh would 'come to', slightly dazed and find himself back in the séance room.

In the early years it took some time for the guides to be able to control the instrument, but as time went on, the rapidity of the changeover increased and was conducted with perfect smoothness.

Often he was controlled, unexpectedly, in all sorts of places; walking along the street, on a tram, in a train, or at a social gathering or party. I recall how, on one occasion he was controlled by Malocca on the Manly Ferry Boat on Sydney Harbour. These sudden controls were made without any effort, and those who may be near at hand were quite unaware that the stranger near them was tranced.

There were many instances where guides or spirit acquaintances moved in and out of his body; just like people poking their friendly heads in and out of an open window. Walsh did not always appreciate this peep-bo technique. One day we three were walking along a Port Melbourne wharf after paying a visit to a big liner. We mingled with other people coming off the ship, and as we stepped on to the wharf, we were met by a few lascars about to board the vessel.

As Walsh passed them he was suddenly controlled and began to speak rapidly in a foreign tongue to one of the lascars. Immediately he, Walsh, was surrounded by five or six of them jabbering excitedly in their own tongue. We found out later that the spirit speaking through Walsh was a lascar who took the opportunity of making himself known to one of his relatives on the wharf. The lascar was not afraid merely excited and intrigued. When Walsh came to he was astonished to find himself surrounded by these lascars all smiling cheerfully and still asking him questions in their language. As he was no longer controlled, and as neither he nor we could understand what they were saying, we just smiled, shook our heads and walked away.

'I wish the guides wouldn't let spirits come through like that', snorted Jones. 'Everyone was looking at us!'

'Well I can't help that,' said the bewildered Walsh, 'if I had known what was going to happen I would have prevented it.'

And this brings us to another aspect of the trance power—how to 'prevent' it. 'During the early stages of Walsh's development Malocca had instructed Jones to tell his friend, how to stop any spirit, including himself, Malocca, from controlling the body.

If he, Malocca, or any other spirit wished to control the medium, and the latter did not want this to happen at that particular time, all Walsh had to do was to put his two thumbs, between the first and second fingers of each hand, then press the thumbs hard. This stopped the flow of magnetism through the instrument and prevented any spirit from taking control. Walsh often did this. It must be understood, however, that when I say 'any spirit from controlling the body', I mean—WITH the doorkeeper's permission.

The spirits referred to that 'popped in and out of the medium', still had to get Malocca's permission. Although a little embarrassing to Walsh at times, it did no harm to him, but was the means of bringing great help and happiness to others, often strangers, to whom the spirit guides spoke. One can imagine the pleasant surprise of the lascar on the wharf who suddenly received a message from a loved relative in the spirit world, in his own tongue, and through the lips of a complete stranger.

So, although Walsh or Jones would get a little peevish sometimes at these unexpected 'visits', they always, on reflection, realised that it was for someone's benefit, and they were satisfied.

13

AN ANGEL OF JOY

> Laughing cheerfulness throws the light of day on all paths of life.
>
> Jean Paul

At this stage I want to relate some of the lighter touches of Walsh's deep trance experiences. God has given us all a sense of humour, stronger in some than in others. Carlyle wrote: 'Humour has justly been regarded as the finest perfection of poetic genius. He who wants it, be his other gifts what they may, has only half a mind.' That is true!

It is a precious gift given to us to lighten the pathway of life when we grow weary or when our minds are darkened by sorrow or worry. The lectures given through Walsh's trance mediumship were of a sublime quality and often imbued with wisdom far beyond that of man's. Those who listened, therefore, had much food for deep and earnest thought. The result was that when the meetings were concluded the conditions in the room were usually deep and profound.

Every member at the séance would be in a more or less serious state of mind. When Walsh came back to consciousness, feeling tired in mind and body, this heavy mental condition surrounding him brought no relief to his weary brain.

We all go through this experience at some time in our everyday life. Perhaps we have been concentrating for hours on a serious problem.

At last, utterly worn out we put aside our task, pick up a comic strip, have a romp with the children or watch a comedy on TV 'to relieve our tired brain'. We often hear of learned professors or solemn judges who lay aside their weighty problems and find relief by reading a 'who-dun-it' novel, and so on.

In like manner, when all kinds of guides had been using his brain, Walsh was tired; he was, perhaps, drained of both physical and mental strength. This made him feel very depressed. He felt at times as if his mind was weighted down by anxiety and all the cares of the world. When he looked around him, all he could see was the circle of sitters, looking serious and thoughtful. Too much profundity was in the air! The solution devised by the guides, was a hearty laugh!

A very bright spirit called Hetty was the one who invariably supplied the laughs. That was her job, and what a wonderful success she made of it! She was one of Walsh's special high guides. Fifty years before, she had died at the age of fourteen. She was a half-caste Maori in New Zealand. She had lived in the poorest of conditions in a Maori shanty town. But Hetty was a very bright soul, even on earth, and when she went back to the spirit world, she progressed very quickly. She eventually reached the higher planes.

She came to the medium a year or so after his first trance experience and used to come through him in two entirely different roles. First, she came through just as herself when on earth, a mischievous, witty Maori girl. But, when she spoke from the higher planes, she expressed herself in a way one would expect her to speak from such a high plane.

An interesting aspect of Hetty's dual roles was that when she came down to help Walsh 'unwind' after a long serious meeting, or when she appeared merely to lift him out of a depressed mood, she would always speak with a marked lisp—a characteristic she bore in her Maori lifetime. When she spoke to Walsh or the meeting in the role of a higher guide delivering spiritual advice and knowledge, Hetty was without lisp and her manner full of poise. All spirits rising high in spiritual planes eventually become perfect, spiritually and mentally, but when they contact the earth again through a flesh and blood instrument they naturally revert to the mannerisms and mode of speech that they possessed then. Hetty, in the flesh, had suffered this slight speech impediment and, in her role as an 'angel of joy', as she was called by the regular sitters, she nearly always spoke as the irrepressible Maori girl, bubbling over with fun and with razor-sharp wit. This wit expressed with a lisp to the voice and accompanied by a mischievous grin added piquancy to everything she said.

Night after night, just before the meetings closed, she would come through and in a few minutes have all the sitters laughing heartily. Hetty was a wonderful, personal guide to Stan, helping him in countless ways to bear the heavy weight that often seemed to be pressing down on him. In his home life she sometimes came to help him in making family decisions, speaking to him clairaudiently. A deep bond of love and understanding existed between them. The old saw: 'A laugh is as good as a tonic', was very apt in Hetty's case. She proved to be a tonic, not only to the instrument himself, but to many who spoke to her throughout the years. Often she would pass on some advice to me, with a grin, and in a way that I could understand, and no one else.

Several times I heard Hetty speak to me in my own home, clairaudiently, with good sensible advice. Throughout the years since then I have heard her inward voice when I most need it. She is not only an 'angel of joy' but an 'angel of common sense'—Bless her!

14

THE POWER OF THOUGHT

> Pray God that the thought of thine heart be forgiven thee
>
> PETER: ACTS 8-22

Florence Barclay a popular English writer, a decade or so ago, received a letter from her daughter criticizing one of the latter's friends. In reply, the mother, wrote, 'My dear, never send an unkind or sneering thought to anyone, no matter who they are—ugly, foolish, quaint or badly dressed. Such thoughts only make them feel uncomfortable or unhappy.'

Professor Jenkinson often gave lectures on the hidden power of thought.

The following are random remarks from one of these talks:

> Not many people realise how much effect thoughts can have on others. We can help them or hurt them, according to the good or evil thoughts we may send towards them.
>
> A man or woman may appear to be friendly, and yet their real thoughts may be antagonistic towards you. You can feel it, but may not be able to put it into words; but the feeling is there, an uneasy, uncomfortable feeling. Unkind thoughts or a feeling of hate towards a person can make them very depressed and unhappy.

Christ knew this, and it is recorded in Matthew, 9:4, that he perceived, or read the thoughts of, the smooth talking Pharisees. The Professor also pointed out how it is possible to sin deeply by thought alone. If a man sends a lustful thought towards the wife of another, or a woman unlawfully desires a man, they have already committed adultery in their hearts. Likewise one can be guilty of theft or corruption in business without enacting the crime.

In this permissive age, pornography in books, films and magazines is looked upon as harmless, providing it is indulged in by adults only. The oft repeated assertions that adults who enjoy such low geared material are 'harming no one else', is a very definite fallacy, as taught by the guides and now being admitted by certain modem scientific and psychological authorities, is a 'force' or 'vibration' which cannot be kept under control by the person generating it.

Expressing the teachings of the guides in modern, technical language, the mind is not only a human 'transmitter' where thought is concerned, but also a 'receiver'. Thus the so-called private pornographic thoughts of adults are unconsciously 'transmitted' and unconsciously 'received' by the young and immature and impressive and could affect their subsequent behaviour adversely, and do untold harm to their morals or even endanger the physical safety of others in society. How many crimes of violence or rapes on children are thus prompted?

> In like manner, true, kindly thoughts can help another person to whom they are sent, and bring an inward feeling of peace or happiness into the soul of that person.
>
> The spontaneous outflowing of a selfless, pure loving thought to anyone in trouble, lifts that troubled person up, and is true prayer in God's sight. God is always very close to the soul of a person who has a selfless, loving heart.

These words of Professor Jenkinson are confirmed today by new scientific knowledge. Russian scientists, in particular, are experimenting with Mental Telepathy to be used in the sphere of Space. Astronauts are being trained to try and pick up thought messages in order to facilitate telepathic communications for space projects of the future.

We can send messages to others by thought, but the important issue is whether these messages uplift or depress the receiver or others who accidentally pick them up, and this depends on the type of messages sent.

On one occasion Professor Jenkinson pointed out that, in the case of mediums' extra sensitive minds, an assault by thought transference can do far more harm to the latter than to the ordinary mind.

On one occasion at Thombury several University students were present at a séance when Jenkinson lectured on the power of human thought. In the course of the talk he referred to this danger to ultra-sensitive minds. If thoughts sent to the latter were forceful, dictatorial or with a strong hate content, the sending of such thoughts was tantamount to hurling a stone at the sensitive's head. A moment or so after these words had been spoken Walsh collapsed on to the floor.

The dim lights were turned up immediately, followed by a confused babble of voices. After a while he recovered, and was helped to his feet.

'Are you alright?' said Jones anxiously. Walsh rubbed his head ruefully.

'I think so. I feel as if I have been hit on the head with something.'

Just then one of the students came forward, looking very foolish. 'I'm afraid I am the cause', he said, 'but I didn't mean to harm Mr Walsh. It was just as much a shock to me as it was to him!'

'What do you mean?' demanded Jones.

'Well, when the Professor said that thoughts were so powerful that if sent forcibly towards anyone, they could be as effective as throwing a stone, I doubted that. Then I said to myself: I wonder if a thought COULD knock him down. So I concentrated...' 'You stupid idiot', burst out Jones, 'you might have...'

'I'm awfully sorry', stammered the student. 'I didn't realise what I was doing I had no idea thoughts could be so effective. Now I'm convinced'.

'A lot of good that is,' growled watchdog Jones.

Here Walsh intervened. 'It's alright, Bert, I understand what the young chap is trying to say. I'm quite certain he didn't mean to harm me. I'm recovered now. Let's forget it.'

Later, Professor Jenkinson explained that the guides allowed this to happen in order to forcibly impress, not only this particular student, but everyone in the room, that harmful thoughts were both dangerous and very wrong. He went on to say that although the medium had been knocked down, Malocca, in this case had protected Walsh from any really harmful effects.

What the guides taught about thought and its effect on others is something that nearly everyone experiences at some time or other. In this world it is now recognized and called mental telepathy. We are all, more or less, influenced by the thoughts of others at some time in our lives. Have we not all at some time been in the company of a person, and after leaving them made the remark: 'It's funny, but all the time I was with so-and-so I felt uncomfortable or uneasy'. I remember a comment made by a woman friend of the wife: 'Somehow, I don't like Mr X. When I am in his company I feel as if I am undressed. He makes me feel somehow embarrassed—why, I don't know.'

Again, I remember a young lady who came to one of our meetings. After it was over she sat beside Miss Grenville, one of the Inner Circle. She was a very unhappy young woman and related her troubles to the former, who listened sympathetically. This same young woman came again to one of the meetings held at Brunswick. On this occasion Miss Grenville was absent. She said to me, 'Will Miss Grenville be coming here to-night?' I said, 'No, she doesn't come to the Brunswick meetings'. Said the young lady, 'It's strange, but when I met her and sat down to talk to her I was very depressed. But when I left to go home all the depression seemed to leave me. She seemed to radiate a sort of peace that I have never experienced before'. I explained to her that Miss Grenville was a very lovable person, who prayed continually for the sick and the sorrowing and was always trying to live up to the teachings of the guides, especially their accent on love your neighbour without ceasing'. The young woman nodded vigorously. 'I can understand now why I felt like that in her presence. She must have been praying for me as I spoke to her!'

15

TO TRAVEL WITHOUT BODY

> I knew a man, whether in the body, or out of the body, I know not...
>
> PAUL: 2 COR.

As time went on and his soul was more developed, Walsh had many strange experiences of a personal nature. Although, on most occasions he knew nothing of what went on when under trance, he was given wisdom and understanding, according to his needs, through the gifts of clairvoyance and clairaudience.

He could hear voices speaking to him. He was shown many scenes of the spirit world and he saw spirit forms near him and near others.

On many occasions he was lifted out of the body and caught up into the higher spheres. On several occasions he was lifted up to meet Christ! A few are privileged from time to time to be lifted up, even while still in the body, to the spiritual realms. It happened not only to biblical personalities like Isaiah, Paul, and others, but to many throughout the years until the present day. To name just a few, there were the Catholic saints, St Teresa of Avila and St Francis of Assisi; and Swedenborg, the Swedish mystic; Sadhu Sunda Singh, the Hindu-Christian missionary; and Madame Melba the Australian singer.

In her autobiography, *Melodies and Memories*, Madame Melba spoke of being lifted up into the spiritual spheres while listening to Wagner's

Parsifal at Hammerstein's Opera House in New York. She explained that the theatre seemed to cease to exist and everything seemed to vanish. 'I was a disembodied spirit, floating in realms of pure music.' She could not determine, 'to what strange sphere' that music transported her. She did remember, however, that the coming back was 'infinitely painful'! Madame Melba had really been lifted up in spirit, out of the body, to the musical spheres of the spirit world. Walsh had these experiences several times. This is what he told me of one occasion:

> I was carried up by Malocca. He seemed to be holding me, and I found myself rising higher and higher. The beautiful things I saw and the scenes of light are beyond description. As I rose I saw wave after wave of spirit faces coming towards me. Many of them I knew. Many spoke to me, or seemed to speak, although it was more like thought forces they sent towards me. Then I found myself drawn towards the Christ. It is very hard to describe Him. At first I seemed to see Him as He would have looked on earth. He seemed to be wearing a sort of coarse brown robe, and as I looked at Him, I felt I had known Him all my life. As a matter of fact I can't possibly describe HOW I felt about Him. The only way I can put it, is to say that when I looked at Him, I felt as if He was my greatest friend, and I loved Him as I have never loved anyone else on earth. But the strange part about it was that I seemed, somehow, to see a higher force, or a hidden power behind the actual figure—there seemed to be behind Him a dazzling light that is impossible to describe. When I came back to this earth, I could have cried with disappointment. I didn't want to come back!'

He went on to say, that, although he was out of the body for only a few minutes, he felt that he had been away for hours. He also said that it is very difficult to give an idea of what the spirit world is like. Everything you see—the spirit forms, the beautiful robes they wear, the wonderful scenes, the flowers, which are far more beautiful than our earth flowers, and everything you look upon—appear to be all in LIGHT—there is nothing material there. Again, you actually do not speak to anyone with your voice, you communicate with each other by thought—thought that somehow has all the beauty and quality of sound.

Another experience which I noted at the time, happened during a meeting of the Inner Circle in 1930. Walsh was controlled by Malocca who said that he had brought into our room a 'visitor' from Belgium. Malocca then left and allowed another man to control the instrument.

This 'control' spoke in his own tongue—which, we understand, was Flemish.

After a while Jones said to him, 'Please try and speak in our tongue, friend'. There was a pause in which the 'visitor' seemed to be looking up at someone, and seeking help; he then began to speak slowly in broken English: 'I come from Dietrich in Belgium. I am—what you say—a deep-trance mediums. I come from a circle of eight peoples. Your medium—he is now in MY body bringing greetings to them, my countrymen. And I bring greetings from my peoples in Dietrich.'

What had happened was that the two deep-trance mediums had exchanged bodies! Walsh's spirit controlling the Belgian's body in Dietrich, and the Belgian's spirit controlling Walsh's body in Melbourne!

When Walsh came to, he said he remembered having found himself sitting in a small dimly lit room. He began to speak, but the people present did not understand what he was saying. He was shown by a spirit guide, hovering just above and in front of him, how to translate the message, so that the Belgian sitters could understand what he was saying. He knew he had been sent to convey greetings from us to these Belgians. Malocca said that these two, Walsh and the 'visitor', were two of very few deep-trance mediums in the world.

'Out of body experiences' are not as extraordinary to people today as they might have been in Walsh's time. 'Astral travel' and the concept of being able to leave the body during sleep or in meditation seems to be an accepted possibility by many—not all of them spiritualists. The important thing to note is the motive for the occurrence in Walsh's case and in that of the saints, and even Madam Melba. Here the motive was altruistic—the experience was meant to be a means of bringing knowledge, comfort and enlightenment to others, and for this reason they would seem to have 'travelled' to very much higher planes than is reported by most 'astral travellers'. Stan Walsh certainly travelled far—reaching the presence of Christ on high. We know that Christ comes often to comfort mankind—but few men are able to rise up to meet Him on the high planes of Eternity.

THE CERTAINTY OF ETERNITY

The painting of Christ

White Bird

Stan with materialised wedding veil

Left to Right. Bert Jones, Stan Walsh, woman unknown, Leslie Danby

Crucifix from Belgian Cathedral

16

APPORTS AND MATERIALIZED GIFTS

> God answers sharp and sudden on some prayers, and thrusts
> the things we have prayed for in our face
>
> ELIZABETH BARRETT BROWNING

The gift of materialization of apports came to Walsh some time in 1921. The psychological definition of materialization is: 'The alleged forming of material objects, or parts of the human body by superhuman means; one of the phenomena studied by psychical research'. Apports are defined as: 'Objects transported by supernormal means from a distance into a definite enclosed space.'

Another Melbourne man, named, Charles Bailey, had that same power. It is a gift given to very few. He was well known in spiritualistic circles and many witnessed his remarkable materializations of all sorts of objects.

One night after one of Walsh's séances a member stated that he had witnessed these apports coming through at one of Bailey's meetings. He said they were produced under strict 'test' conditions, and had no doubt as to their genuine nature. He spoke in high terms of Bailey's integrity and character. Nevertheless, several members found it hard to believe that such a gift could possibly be genuine. As if in answer, Malocca suddenly controlled Walsh and told them that Bailey's gift was a reality. He added that if Walsh and the sitters prayed earnestly for this gift, it might come to their medium. So they did.

Before going any further it might be appropriate to draw attention to references made in the Bible regarding materializations. Among the most striking instances are, Jacob's encounter with an Angel materialized into flesh and blood, and Moses' materializations before Pharoah, rods turned into serpents, a clean hand turned into a leprous one, and water changed into blood; Elijah was taken up in a chariot of fire; the materialization of fire on Mount Carmel. A search of the Old Testament will reveal many more. The most famous examples, however, are the ones relating to Jesus. At Cana where water turned into wine; the materialization of enough loaves and fishes to feed a multitude; the silver coin, at Christ's direction, found in the mouth of a fish by Peter, and the greatest of all—the materialization of Jesus resurrected and the subsequent ease with which He in His resurrected body passed and re-passed through solid, wooden doors. So what I am describing is nothing new. Materialization is a gift as old as the Bible itself.

Some months after Malocca's remarks about materialization, an announcement was made by one of the high guides that, at the next Tuesday night's meeting, some feathers would be materialized. Later, Mrs Lehman remarked, I wouldn't be surprised if the feathers to be materialized are black'.

'How do you know?' asked Jones.

'Because I saw, clairvoyantly, several black feathers sticking out of Stan's hair, just as the guide made the announcement.'

At the next meeting, and half way through the night, there was a sudden fluttering sound and the sitters saw tiny black feathers floating down from the ceiling. They immediately stopped singing, and got down on their knees, excitedly picking them up, as they fell to the floor.

From then onwards apports began to appear, often at most unexpected places and times. Jones told me that one night he and Walsh happened to be walking down the North end of Elizabeth Street in the City, when suddenly Walsh was controlled, he gave a choking sort of gasp, his right hand was thrown high up in the air, and Malocca gasped, 'Here it is!' Then the hand was brought down and there it was! 'It' was a large, wooden crucifix about twelve inches long! Jones said it happened at about nine-thirty p.m. There were very few in the street. It happened so quickly that nobody seemed to notice. 'We could hardly believe it was true,' said Jones, 'but there it was in his hand!' Many years later that same crucifix was given to the writer, and he has it to this day.

Crucifixes of all sorts and sizes were materialized from then on. Mrs Martin told me that on one occasion she asked the Egyptian guide,

APPORTS AND MATERIALIZED GIFTS

Vashti, why so many crucifixes came through, His reply was that many spiritualists in Melbourne, at that time, had denied Christ and that His name was no longer mentioned at their spiritual services.

That was true. For a few months after I first met Walsh I went to many of these spiritualist churches, but was disappointed by the quality of the services, the obvious fortune-telling atmosphere and the low standard of mediumship, which in many cases was obviously false. Prayers were made to 'The Pure Spirit of Love', or, 'The Great Cosmic Spirit', and so on. NO mention was made of Christ. I remember remarking this lack to one of their leaders, in those early days, and he said: 'Oh, we don't want any of that 'Gentle Jesus' stuff, let them keep that for Sunday Schools and Churches!' Since then—this was in the late 'twenties—several spiritualistic churches have opened up in Melbourne which DO recognise Christ as the Son of God.

> Vashti announced at this time, that these images of Christ on the Cross were sent to impress upon all who received them, including some sincere spiritualists, that CHRIST SHOULD BE RECOGNISED AT ALL SPIRITUAL SERVICES.

When the first tidings of Walsh's materialized gifts and apports came to the ears of spiritualists in various churches, some declared that the apports must have been 'stolen' by the guides. Some of Walsh's followers were upset by these charges, but Malocca reassured them, by explaining that everything 'brought down' into the séance room had been irretrievably lost or buried and could never be recovered by normal human means.

When I joined the Inner Circle I witnessed many materializations at Mrs Martin's home. One of them took three or four weeks before it came through—but it was shown to us before it finally came. Mrs Martin's daughter, Grace, was engaged to be married. The Tuesday after the announcement of the engagement, Malocca stated that the guides were going to materialize her wedding veil. It would take some time, but with patience it would eventually come. From then onward, each Tuesday night, we noticed a fine, filmy, cloudy substance begin to hover around the ceiling. One night, without warning, there was a peculiar rushing sound just like the faint flapping of a host of birds' wings. Then it fell down over our heads! A beautiful wedding veil, light as down, and magnificently embroidered. I have a photo of this veil in my study drawer, and another photo of Walsh holding the veil.

I received a crucifix for myself which had personal significance and which I was told was recovered by the guides from the ruins of a Belgian cathedral destroyed during World War I, and since then the site of a new church. This is how it came: There had been some suggestion by the General Manager at our office that I should be transferred to their New South Wales factory (just opened) to install and organise an office staff. I was very reluctant to leave Melbourne and my friends, and break off all association with the spiritual work I had engaged in during the last two years.

While the question was being debated on high managerial levels, I was asked by Malocca, one Tuesday night, to step into the séance room with just Walsh and Jones, as the guides had something to say. We three sat down on chairs and Professor Jenkinson immediately came through and said that it was not the Will of God that I leave the Inner Circle. I would find that the final decision would be to keep me in Melbourne.

He added that it was planned that we three continue to be bound together in friendship until the work of God was finished through the medium. He continued by saying a certain guide, a Father O'Brien, who had been a Catholic priest on earth, had brought along a crucifix retrieved from the ruins of a Belgian cathedral. God had given this priest power to materialise the cross and give it to me as a symbol of this binding friendship, between Walsh, Jones and myself.

Jenkinson then asked us to bring each right hand together. He took Jones' hand and placed it under Walsh's. He then took my right hand and placed it firmly on the flat, empty hand of Walsh. So there we were! The three right hands clasped together tightly, one on top of the other, with Walsh's hand in the middle—empty—because I was grasping it. But, as the Professor continued speaking, I felt something hard forming between the palm of my hand and Walsh's. 'And this,' said the Professor, 'is the symbol sent to bind you three together—and no man can break this link.'

As he left the instrument our hands were still clasped tightly together—with a crucifix in between! When Walsh opened his eyes he stared in astonishment at us. I took my hand off his and showed him the cross, about seven inches by four. We were all amazed at the smoothness with which it came—in the full light of the room. That cross still hangs on the wall of my study.

'Old timers' will remember an actress of the silent film days called Olive Thomas. She died in the late twenties. She spoke several times

APPORTS AND MATERIALIZED GIFTS

to theatrical folk who came on Sunday nights. She took a great fancy to Mrs Martin's daughter, Grace. The latter had many talks to her through direct voice conversations.

One night she told Grace that she was going to give her a blue, silk shawl that belonged to her on earth. Some weeks later we three came along as usual on Tuesday night. It was a cold night and Mrs Martin had a roaring fire in the room. We sat by the fire, just the four of us. As we sat chatting, Walsh was 'taken away', and there was Malocca. He asked us to put out the light. 'We bring something quick!' he said.

We hurriedly switched off the light. We could see everything in a dim way by the light of the fire. I will explain later why dim lights are needed at times not only for materializations but also for direct voice trumpet séances.

In the meantime Malocca, controlling Walsh's body, was almost dancing around the room on tiptoe with both hands stretched high above the medium's head. We could see a vaguely formed cloud just out of his reach.

'Sing! Sing!' he cried, 'it help me bring it!'

So we sang. It was the hymn, 'There is Power'. Everyone sang in a different key. It sounded awful, but we kept on manfully while Malocca kept reaching up to grasp or touch the ethereal cloudy substance almost within reach. Then slowly it started to descend upon the outstretched hands of our guide. There was a loud cry of triumph from Malocca, the medium's hands touched the filmy cloud and it immediately turned into a large, bright blue, silk shawl of superb workmanship.

We turned on the light and crowded around Malocca, proudly holding the shawl in his hands. 'This is what Olive-Thomas-girl promise your Grace-girl', he said to Mrs Martin.

When Grace came home that night her delight and gratitude to Walsh was worth all the strain he had undergone during the materialization.

In later years we used to hold a meeting at a French medium's home in East Brunswick. Her name was Madame Gisel. These meetings were held at her home every second Saturday. She was an inspirational medium herself. She was a bright, warm-hearted woman, sincere and devout. One night a Chinese mandarin came through and told us that he lived on this earth five thousand years ago. He came from the eleventh, the highest plane of light and gave a wonderful lecture on spiritual matters. At the conclusion of his talk he said he had brought a Chinese fan for each sitter and that these would be found at the feet of each one after the meeting. When the lights were turned up, there they were—beautifully coloured fans—to the delight of everyone in the room.

One weekend members of the Inner Circle had been invited to Mrs Lehman's home at Panton Hills, an old country farmhouse.

On the Saturday afternoon we went for a walk in the bush. As we stood at the top of the hill, Walsh was controlled by Malocca who pointed down the hill to a clump of gum trees growing almost in the form of a circle.

'The guides say they want to hold meeting there tonight—among those trees. You come! I show you!'

With that, he began to run like a hare. It was a sight to see! The frail body of Walsh, leaping and running, clearing two or three post and rail fences, one after the other, like a steeple chaser!

'Gosh, I've got to catch him,' gasped Bert Jones, 'Stan's legs can't keep up that pace!' But they did; then as we watched, we saw a flaring red robe flying behind him.

At last he stopped in the middle of a natural arena with the gum trees surrounding him. When we arrived, panting, we found that Armah Singh, the Hindu seer had taken Malocca's place. A bright, red robe was now draped neatly around the body of the medium. It had been materialized whilst he was running!

That night, as requested, a meeting was held in that special spot, within the circle of the trees, under perfect conditions.

It is interesting to note that 'perfect conditions' were not always possible in the city, even in those days. Looking backwards from an age when pollution and over large cities pose a real threat to man's progression, this episode, recounted, takes on an allegorical dimension.

Over the years all sorts of articles were brought down. Far more of these occurrences took place than can be recorded in this book, but for the interest of readers two of the most curious apports to arrive are explained here:

> There was a dagger, secreted within a fan, which originally belonged to Mary, Queen of Scots. It has the appearance of a folded fan, but was actually a camouflaged dagger sheath. This was materialized and given to Miss Grenville, who, in turn, gave it to me. I still have it.

> There was the night when 'White Bird', Malocca's Indian squaw, came through singing a lullaby in the Indian tongue. We could see her, in the dim light, singing. As she did, she stretched the instrument's

hands above his head, and as she brought them down, we noticed that she was holding something in 'her' hands. She laughed and then proceeded to put the article on 'her' head. 'Look!' she said—and there was a leather headgear of the kind worn by Indian squaws. I still have this in my possession.

As the last surviving member of the Inner Circle, Walsh's original small group which was kept as the nucleus or prayer-power centre of his spiritual work, I now find my study a veritable sanctuary for the protection and care of these relics that were so precious to us.

Some of Walsh's staunchest followers over the years were very sceptical when they first attended his meetings. Bearing in mind what they saw, it is quite natural that they doubted. They were honest sceptics with open minds, however, and Walsh was always anxious that these honest doubters be convinced. Carlyle once said that 'Honest scepticism is not an end but a beginning'. Indeed that type of scepticism does not close the mind; it can be the start of a new belief.

Materialization of apports is, understandably, very difficult to accept as genuine. It appears to be too much like the magician's rabbit-out-of-the-hat technique. However, there were a few instances where honest doubts about materializations were the forerunners of firm belief.

Mrs Hanger was a well known inspirational medium in Melbourne. She heard about the apports. She frankly admitted to Walsh that she could not possibly see how these apports could come. So she was invited one Sunday night to a meeting. During the evening Malocca came through, took her by the hand, and led her right under the dimmed electric light. He held her open hand right under the light, where every one could see it. He then told her to close it tightly, and quickly. She did so, and gave a gasp of surprise. She found herself holding a beautifully made crucifix. She was convinced.

Now and then séances were held at Mrs May's home in North Melbourne, usually on Fridays. One night twelve of us were sitting at a direct-voice, trumpet séance. The room was dimly lit, and it would have been impossible for anyone to have crawled or walked around the room without being seen.

During the evening Vashti came through. He said that each one of the sitters would receive a symbol of their faith in Jesus Christ as the Son of God. 'When the lights are turned up,' he said, 'look down at your feet.'

Later under full light, we saw our gifts. At the feet of each one of us was a small crucifix.

It was suggested to me, by an outsider, to whom I related the above, that perhaps the medium had quietly thrown the crucifixes at the feet of each one. Even if he had thrown them down as suggested, I would have clearly seen it, as I was sitting right next to him!

Mrs Beames was another who heard about these materializations with misapprehension. She had not visited Walsh's circle for many years and she had had no experience with apports. She, too, doubted.

One day she invited Walsh to have lunch with her at her Port Melbourne home. After lunch she asked him to explain about the apports. He said, 'I can't. I don't understand it myself.' Then Malocca interrupted. There in broad daylight, he materialized a large white feather and put it into Mrs Beames' hand. She took it in astonishment. Said he, 'You bite on quill of feather, see what you feel'. Puzzled, she did so, and felt something hard inside the quill. She slit the quill with a pen knife. Inside was a very small gold object in the shape of a heart. 'How did it get inside the quill?' she asked in amazement. Malocca explained that it was dematerialized at the same time as the feather, and then placed inside the quill while both were in a dematerialized state. When materialized again, the heart was inside the quill, which explained the mystery.

It was always asked: How is it possible to materialize these apports? Angus Du Font lectured several times on this phenomenon. He began with references to the great strides scientists were then making with the atom, and even more that shall be discovered to amaze the world very soon'. He was referring, of course, to the 'nuclear development, the splitting of the atom', which was still a long way off when this lecture was given. He also referred to the fact that there is no such thing as solid matter. The varying density of all types of matter is conditioned by the speed of the atoms contained within the molecules of any given object.

Articles were dematerialized by scientific minds in the spirit world. They used the peculiar magnetic power contained within the body of the medium, in conjunction with the 'spiritual power' which they controlled when dematerializing objects.

These combined forces were used to speed up the atoms of the article in question until it was no longer visible to the human eye, nor tangible to human touch.

In its dematerialized state the article was then carried from where it was originally found, beyond all human access, to the place where it was to be again materialized. This dematerialized article, when brought into sudden contact with the magnetic force issuing from the medium's hands, reduced the stepped up speed of the atoms, to the original rate so that the article became visible again, and composed of dense matter once more.

This swift change did suggest magic to some but of course, it was not so.

It was certainly no mystery to those dwelling in the world of spirit—just one of those things that the scientific mind of man had yet to discover, but would one day—with an important 'breakthrough' as a beginning.

A very simple explanation of materialization of apports is possible by referring to the conversion of water into steam by heat. It is then possible to bring the steam back to water by bringing it into contact with a cold plate. We were told that in a sense, the materializing medium could be regarded as a human 'cold plate', used by the guides to produce these apports.

17

AUTOMATIC PAINTING

> Painting is the intermediate between a thought and a thing
>
> COLERIDGE

We now come to the gift of automatic painting, and materialization of colours. Stan Walsh, in his conscious state, could not draw a straight line although his brother, Cecil, who died sometime earlier, could paint fairly well.

This painting phenomena was developed in our meetings by Professor Jenkinson. His hobby was painting when on earth, and he thoroughly understood the subject. He could control Walsh and paint portraits of those on the other side of life. He did not use watercolour or oil-paint or any conventional colouring matter; he simply materialized the colours through the medium's finger tips!

Jenkinson explained this process several times. He said that every flower sends out vibrations which draw to it various colours out of the atmosphere—colours with corresponding vibrations. A plant with a vibration rate corresponding to red, would draw red colour from the atmosphere. Another plant, with a different rate of vibration inherent in itself, could draw from the atmosphere, yellow, and so on.

As a glass prism breaks up the sun's rays in the atmosphere into all the colours of the spectrum, so do these blooms draw from the sun's rays, by their various vibrations, certain colours sensitive to that particular flower.

In the springtime the air is full of these colours—unseen. On the principle applying to plants, the medium, Walsh, was gifted with the same magnetic vibrations which could draw colours of every hue from the atmosphere.

Jenkinson said that the magnetic force drawing colour from the air radiated from the right breast of Walsh's body. These colour forces passed down his right arm, and as they reached the finger tips were immediately materialized into paint when they contacted the atmosphere which exuded from his fingers on to the canvas, paper or satin upon which Jenkinson, through the medium, was working.

He added that the materialization of colours is somewhat similar to the action of a ray of light, which is only visible—in clear air—when it strikes a reflecting surface. In the same manner, the dematerialized paints were only visible when they touched these canvases, etc.

Different colours were produced through each finger. It was not intended that the fingers should touch the surface of the painting material. Sometimes this happened, by accident, and in such cases a definite blotch of colour would show up in the painting.

I witnessed, together with many others, the transfer of colours on to paper. Professor Jenkinson, or sometimes the spirit of the medium's brother, Cecil Walsh, when controlling the medium, would take an ordinary pencil or a pen and using the medium's hands, sketch the outline of the face or figure he was working upon. After the pen or pencil outline was completed, he would cause the medium to start to massage the fingers of each hand, with a rapid washing motion, one hand over the other. This was done in order to release, or set in motion, the flow of magnetism through the fingers which was needed to materialize the colours.

Then he would hold the two hands of the medium over the sketch and shake the fingers deftly and swiftly over every portion of the outline. As he did this, one could see the colours forming on the portrait. Finally, it would be finished, in vivid colours—life-like and clear.

Throughout those years an endless profusion of portrait paintings were completed—mostly of guides or spirit personalities. Nearly all of them were the work of Professor Jenkinson, but some were completed by Walsh's brother, Cecil.

One of the portraits drawn and coloured by Cecil was for me. My still born baby daughter who had died with her mother, my first wife, was sketched by him when she had grown to be six years old in the spirit world. At the bottom of the portrait he printed neatly in pencil: 'Little Winnie, aged six, come to guide her father through life.'

Paintings given to sitters throughout the years were of Red Indian guides, Hindu and Persian guides, many of the very high guides, such as Ruth, Naomi, Mary Magdalene, the Holy Mother and many portraits of the Christ, as seen in the spirit world.

There was one outstanding painting of the Christ, which was framed and hung in Mrs Martin's lounge room for many years. It was admired by all. Many art students examined it from time to time, and were often intrigued by the strange blending of colours, and the elusive shades procured. This, also, was first sketched in pencil, with the colours as usual sent through the fingertips. It took half an hour to complete. When Mrs Martin died, the painting was left to me, being the last surviving member of the Inner Circle. It now hangs in my study.

The painting of Christ

Many sitters brought along black and white photographs and asked Walsh to colour them. This he would do, under trance, in their presence.

One night vivacious, blonde haired Mrs McIntosh, a regular Sunday night member, brought along an enlarged black and white photograph of herself in a beautiful gold frame, complete with glass. Before the meeting started she asked Walsh if he would colour it for her. He agreed. So she turned over the back of the framed photo and began to tear off the brown paper holding the photo to the frame, so that he could get to the actual picture. But Jenkinson bobbed up through the medium and told her not to bother. Mrs McIntosh gasped in surprise. The Professor controlling the medium, took the photograph from her, and in her presence and others, including myself, began to colour the photograph with the medium's fingertips through the glass!

As the colour stained fingers shook just above the framed photograph, we saw, appearing through the glass, the pink coming on to the cheeks, the red on the lips, golden yellow tint her hair, and blue slowly appear in the eyes. When he had finished, there before our astonished eyes, was this perfectly coloured photograph of Mrs McIntosh, painted through the glass!

Jenkinson explained that it was the usual technique of 'materialization through the fingers, followed by dematerialization through the glass, and final materialization when the colours touched the surface of the photo'.

Many of the sitters would bring along handkerchiefs, pieces of white canvas or white satin to have their loved ones or their guides painted on these articles. On one occasion Walsh asked me if I had a piece of black satin. 'No, but I can get a piece', I said.

'Well, bring it along next week as I think they want to paint a portrait of your guide, Red Chief.' I did this, and in due course it was operated on by Jenkinson.

The strange part about this was the fact that when I first saw the portrait of Red Chief, although I had never seen him before, I felt that I had known him all my life.

Several others who also received portraits of their guides had the same strange experience. Jenkinson explained to us one night that, although the conscious mind may not be aware of the continual guidance and presence of a guide, the soul was always aware of a guide's presence. Thus, when seeing his or her face for the first time, there comes an indescribable feeling of deep love, and conviction that one has known the guide intimately all one's life.

AUTOMATIC PAINTING

Another strange feature about the painting gift was that on many occasions the paintings were produced instantaneously. Here is one instance:

A middle aged man named Ernie Arnold was brought along one night. He was an honest, down to earth person; tall and serious, with solemn brown eyes and a grim look about the mouth which gave the impression of one constantly dotting i's and crossing t's with meticulous care.

After his first spiritual experience in which his father spoke to him and gave messages of an evidential nature, Ernie was very impressed, but puzzled. He asked 'Could I come again?' Said Walsh, 'Yes, by all means.'

And so he began to come regularly to the Sunday night sittings. Then he heard about the strange paintings executed by the medium, without brush or paint, through the tips of his fingers. He was shown various portraits of guides by sitters. One night he ventured to ask if he could bring along a handkerchief of his own, as the others used to do, so that his guide, whom he had been told previously was 'Blazing Arrow', a Red Indian, could be painted on it.

Consent was given, and on the following Sunday he came along with a huge handkerchief which looked like a miniature table cloth. In each corner of the handkerchief he had printed, in black Indian ink, his initials, so as to ensure that the handkerchief was not switched.

He asked Walsh if he minded the inky precautions which he had taken.

Walsh smiled and said, 'Not in the least'.

'Shall I put it on the floor?' 'Oh, no, just keep it in your pocket. The guides will tell you when they want it,' said Walsh.

During the evening a Red Indian controlled the medium and walked towards Ernie. Standing in front of him with arms folded and head thrown back—a typical Red Indian stance— the guide said, 'Me, Blazing Arrow, your guide'. His voice was deep, harsh and reverberating. 'You want'em picture on your hankumchief? Give it me!' Ernie took out the handkerchief and handed it over.

What I am going to relate could not have taken more than a few seconds. Blazing Arrow opened the handkerchief. He then held it at two ends—we could see him quite clearly in the dim light. Then he began to flap the handkerchief furiously up and down in the air for a few moments, and with a triumphant shout threw it into Ernie's lap. 'You look 'em at it now. See on it my face!'

The lights were turned up for a moment and Ernie stared in amazement at the powerful face of an Indian Chief wearing full headdress!

Then he carefully scrutinized the corners of the handkerchief. His initials in black were there all right! 'It's certainly my handkerchief, he muttered. 'It's astounding'.

Later in the evening Jenkinson explained to the astonished Ernie, and other sitters, how it was done. He said that the painting of his guide had already been completed in the spirit world. It was a dematerialized painting. The latter was placed in front of Blazing Arrow, holding the handkerchief. When the latter was furiously flapped up and down through the dematerialized portrait, it was instantaneously materialized as it touched the handkerchief.

Ernie was convinced beyond doubt. This kindly 'Doubting Thomas' became one of Walsh's most ardent followers. He remained a regular member of the Sunday night meetings right to the end, with a great respect, not only for the guides and their teachings, but also for the man, Walsh.

A few years after meeting Walsh I was asked to assist at the South Melbourne Presbyterian Mission in Dorcas Street, South Melbourne. I began as a Sunday Kindergarten Teacher, and after a few weeks, I was asked by the Deaconess if I would take over as Leader of the Kindergarten. 'You seem to have a way with children', she said. I suppose my experience in entertaining children in my days as a professional ventriloquist, was the reason. I agreed. The Leader's task was to take the opening service with the combined 'Kinder' classes. It began by telling a story, followed by simple prayer, and then a hymn. The children then dispersed to their various classes. They used to sit on small, low chairs in a big circle around me.

One night Professor Jenkinson came through at a meeting and said to me, 'Friend, I would like to paint a portrait of Jesus and give it to you. I suggest that you frame it and take to your Sunday Kindergarten. At the end of the opening service before the last hymn, let each of the children take turns in holding this picture up for all the other children to see; then ask them to sing, Jesus Loves Me, while the picture is held in front of them. The memory of His image will sink into their souls, and in years to come it will vitally influence their lives and advance them spiritually.' In a few days time Walsh brought this painting to me. It was painted on a piece of white silk. I had it framed and took it to the Sunday Kindergarten. Holding this picture and singing the hymn, Jesus Loves Me, became a part of the ritual of this service. Each week the children would eagerly clamour with upraised hands to hold it.

The Professor remarked some time later, 'By constantly adhering to this practice in the service, Jesus is able to silently plant the seed of love and goodness in the hearts of these little ones—a seed which one day will bear fruit in their lives'.

There is an old and obviously well tested saying in the Catholic Church, attributed to one of their saints, that declares: 'Give me a child until it is six years old, and you can do what you like with it after that!'

18

DIRECT VOICE COMMUNICATION

> The border between the credible and the incredible has not only become vague, but the credible is obviously increasing, and the incredible shrinking
>
> G. K. CHESTERTON

Throughout the ages all classes of people have heard voices speaking to them from the world of the spirit. Apart from the saints, let us quote a few celebrities during the last century: Florence Nightingale, William Penn, George Fox, John Bunyan, Elizabeth Fry, the prison reformer, John Wesley, David Livingstone, Dr Flynn of the Australian Inland and a host of others. In addition there are many ordinary people whose probity and good sense are beyond doubt, who are not spiritualists but who have heard voices speaking to them—inward, but unmistakable, voices.

We also know, of course, that some mentally ill people think they hear voices. But we are not speaking of these or of the experiences of drug users.

In the life of Abraham Lincoln it is related that as a boy he was one day walking through the forest. On seeing a bird, he picked up a stone to throw at it. Suddenly he heard an inward voice say, 'Put down that stone!' He did.

Later he spoke to his mother about the incident. 'Where did that voice come from?' he asked her. His mother replied, 'Abie, some people might call it the voice of conscience, but really, my boy, it was the voice of your guardian angel.'

I also recall reading an incident in the life of a man called Dickinson, a member of the Oxford Group in London. He was then a successful Direct businessman, and in a talk he gave to the group he said, 'When I was a young man, I was jobless, hungry, down and out. In a fit of deep depression I was about to throw myself over Hungerford Bridge into the Thames River, when, without warning I heard an inward voice distinctly say: 'Buck up, old chap!' That voice put new life into me. It gave me courage to go on, and eventually I got a job and worked my way up to where I am now.'

I remember a dour Scots uncle of my wife's, a veteran of the First World War, who once told me of a peculiar incident that happened to him in a small French village where his regiment was staying. It was his custom to walk from the farmhouse where he was billeted to a seat built under a large sheltered crucifix in the village square and there sit for a while. One day he was making his way towards it when he heard a voice say, 'Hughie, stop!' He did so in astonishment, and gazed round but not a soul was in sight. Thinking it was his imagination he shrugged his shoulders and kept on walking. Again he heard the voice say, 'Hughie, stop!' He stopped in amazement, hesitated, and heard the voice say again, 'Go back!'

'That was enough for me', recalled the uncle. 'I turned and walked back to the farm house, and then it happened. I heard a low whistling noise, then a terrific boom; a shell exploded right at the foot of the crucifix and blew it to pieces. It would have been the end of me if I had kept going'.

That was his first and only experience of being 'ordered about by a voice', as he put it. This relative was not given to flights of fancy. He was a very shrewd, hard headed man and I believed him. When I related this to a friend he remarked, 'Why doesn't God send voices to warn other people of danger who go on and lose their lives?' I replied, repeating what the guides had taught, 'This person's span of life was not complete, as planned by God before he was born'.

We must remember, however, that all the 'voices' just referred to were 'inward'—in each case it was a subjective experience.

During the last few decades, however, it has been possible for anyone to hear voices from the ethereal realms, if they so wish it. This has

DIRECT VOICE COMMUNICATION

been made possible by the advent of a new and previously unknown substance called ectoplasm. The psychological definition of this word is: 'substance assumed to emanate from the medium, at a spiritualistic séance'.

There have been, and still are, many genuine direct voice séances which are held in various homes throughout the world. The discovery of ectoplasm has made this possible—that is, the experience of voices heard outside of the hearers. The hearing of these materialized voices has been an objective experience.

These audible spirit voices depend upon ectoplasm being available in the séance room. One does not have to be a clairvoyant to see it. In appearance it looks like a light, smokey vapour, or fog-like substance. It issues from various parts of the medium. In Walsh's case it emerged from the pit of the stomach.

Albert Einstein was once asked if he thought there could be any actual credence attached to the claim that ectoplasm issues from the human body. Einstein replied, 'There are certain human emanations which we do not yet understand. Remember how sceptical people were about electric currents and invisible waves? Science is still in its infancy'.

When a direct voice séance is being held, the bulk of the ectoplasm comes from the medium, but everyone in the room contributes a certain amount. All humans possess this ectoplasmic force, but a direct voice medium has far more. As the meeting gets under way, the smaller contributions from each sitter are linked with the greater bulk issuing from the medium, which forms one 'whole' or 'bank'. Spiritual guides then work on this 'bank' and mould or fashion it into semi-materialized hands, which move the megaphone around the room, and a human voice box and larynx to enable spirits to speak aloud.

But the voices are soft, and although they are strengthened by the sound waves of singing or music, one still has to strain one's ears to hear what they say. Hence the need of a megaphone or trumpet, which is carried around and used by spirit hands, materialized. It is through these megaphones that the spirit voice is amplified.

It has often been asked how ectoplasm is released from the human body? The answer is, by the earnest, sincere desire of all the sitters expressed in unison in their silent prayers. This means that each sitter must possess a sympathetic, open mind. There is another name for it — a theological one — FAITH.

Because direct voice meetings have to be held in almost total darkness it is often asserted by those who have never studied, or witnessed, or earnestly looked into the subject, that the medium needs to operate in the dark, so he can manipulate the trumpet, and speak through it himself.

In reply it is necessary to point out that semi-darkness, but not actual darkness, is necessary for ectoplasm to function; it cannot be materialized, or function, in bright light. It has to be strengthened or formed in darkness in the same way as a photographic film is developed. Bright light causes it to disintegrate.

The name 'ectoplasm' was given to the substance of materialized forms appearing at séances by the authority on psychic research, Dr Charles Richet. *In his book, Thirty Years of Psychical Research*, Dr Richet explains that the material he so named actually emerges from the body of the medium. A chemical analysis of ectoplasm was made by a co-worker of Dr Richet, Baron A. von Schrenck Notzing, a German physician who specialized in psychiatry and psychical research and who had spent over thirty-five years conducting séance experiments. His analysis, using a small piece of the material which he obtained with the full cooperation and permission of the medium, was that it was: 'Colourless, slightly cloudy, thread-like almost to the point of fluid, without smell and with traces of cell detritus and sputum. It left a whitish deposit and had a slightly alkaline reaction.' Under the microscope it was revealed to have: 'Numerous skin discs, some sputum-like bodies, numerous granulates of the mucous membrane, numerous minute particles of flesh, traces of potash sulphozyansaurem'.

In the book, *This Is Spiritualism* by Maurice Barbenell, ectoplasm is explained as being ideoplastic by nature and capable of being moulded to 'manufacture' the equivalent of a human body or part thereof. Its relationship to materialization is similar to that of protoplasm in all material forms of life—the essential ingredient of life on this planet. Although non-material in its primal state, ectoplasm is somehow compounded by 'spirit chemists' until it assumes the equivalent of the human body, with a pounding heart, pulse beats and warm, solid hands. It becomes a form that breathes, walks and talks and is apparently complete, even to the fingernails.

Ectoplasm comes out of the medium's solar plexus, or his nose or ears or other bodily orifices. Infrared and flash photographs have been taken of mediums with ectoplasm pouring forth from them—and also of the actual materialized figures. Some of these pictures even show the figures holding a trumpet or lifting an instrument. Photographs of this nature have been made in many different research centres in most continents of the world.

I would point out that although Walsh's meetings were held in the dark, the room was NOT in total darkness. This was because all the articles to be used in the séance were dabbed with luminous paint. The usual articles used in his meetings were, in addition to the megaphone, a banjo which spirit fingers could play, a large luminous crucifix which was often carried around the room by the same spirit hands, and a toy piano for children to play.

By the collected dim light of the luminous paint on these objects it was possible to see everybody. No one could move from their chairs or even move their arms without being seen.

The luminous paint on these articles was there for an obvious reason— so they could be seen floating up and down and around the room quite clearly.

In practically all cases those who came along to the direct voice meetings were earnest, thoughtful people. Many came with sad hearts after the loss of someone they loved; so for them, the experience of hearing the voice of their guide or those of relatives was indeed a great joy. For these there was real meaning in Dickinson's remark to the Oxford Group: 'That voice put new life into me. It gave me courage to carry on'.

19

A THOUSAND SPIRIT VOICES

Love's voice sounds just as sweet coming from the lips of a beggar as it does from a king

DECKER

Over the years I kept notes of incidents from many of the meetings. Sometimes I wrote down the month and year. Here are just a few, representative of over five hundred direct voice meetings—and more than a thousand different spirit voices. The same voices came through on many different occasions of course.

June 1930: My brother's wife was taken to Fairfield hospital seriously ill. The doctors said there was little hope of recovery. The following night Win, my late wife, spoke to me through the megaphone, and asked me to give a message to my brother. She said: 'Doris is not as bad as the doctors think. She will recover, but it will be slow. She is weak inwardly and will have a struggle to rid herself of the complaint. Pray for her recovery. Tell Ossie she WILL get well and spend many happy years with him and the children'. She did recover eventually and lived for another thirty-two years.

August 1932: Mrs Eskdale asked if she could bring along a friend. She did not give his name and he was not introduced to the medium, nor to anyone else. During the night the megaphone was whisked into the air and a man's voice began to sing the Marseillaise vigorously in French. Immediately Mrs Eskdale's friend joined in, singing also in French. Then followed an exciting conversation in the same language. After the meeting the visitor explained to Walsh that the spirit voice he spoke to was that of his brother. The giving of names and intimate information by this brother in French had convinced him.

October 1932: One night a heavy, wooden chair was in the room. A certain Major McArthur suggested that it be put in the circle to see what happened. Daubs of luminous paint were placed on it. During the night it suddenly shot to the ceiling. The meeting was held at Madame Gisel's home, an old fashioned place with a lofty ceiling, twelve feet high. Then the chair began to tap gently on the ceiling, moving from one end of the room to the other. The Major asked, 'Friend, could you bring the chair down towards me and let me touch it?' He wanted to make sure it was the same chair. At once it came down and the tips of the wooden legs tapped him gently on the knees, while he touched the chair with his hands. He was satisfied.

November 1932: The hero of this story was a medical man. He was a well-known Collins Street specialist. He came along one Sunday by special invitation. He saw the trumpet move around the room and heard the spirit voices speak to him. When the lights went up he took out a large white handkerchief from his pocket, lifted up the trumpet, and wiped the handkerchief carefully around both ends of it, inside and out.

Asked why he did this, he said, 'I want to get this sticky substance adhering to the trumpet analysed'.

It appeared subsequently that he had an idea that the 'sticky substance' was human saliva. Later, analysis proved that it was not human saliva. He was convinced that the phenomena was genuine, but he just couldn't understand how such things could be. He was told that what he wiped off the trumpet was ectoplasm.

'Well', he said with a smile, 'It may be what you call ectoplasm, but it certainly was not human saliva—so I am satisfied that no human voice spoke through that trumpet'.

March 1933: A young man, a stranger, was brought along one night by Ernie Arnold. Later, the spirit of his father spoke to him. During the conversation the young man said, 'If it is really you, Dad, tell me what your second name is'. His father replied, 'Ichabod'. He was given other definite proof by the intimate family matters discussed. 'But what impressed me most', he said, 'Was the name "Ichabod". I am a stranger to you all, and I don't suppose there is one in ten thousand who has such an unusual name as that!'

April 1933: One night, Mrs McIntosh brought along a steel guitar.

During the night, a little boy in spirit called 'Peter', took the guitar and asked the sitters to sing 'O, Love, that will not let me go'. But no one could remember the tune. After a few false starts and weird noises, the guitar hovering near the ceiling, began to play the tune, and then everyone joined in.

June 1933: A middle aged woman from Brighton was brought along by Mrs Violet May, a regular sitter. The stranger had a long and earnest conversation with her husband in spirit. She was very happy with what she saw and heard. On her next visit she spoke to me. She explained, I told a brother of mine that I had spoken to my husband, who gave me his name, and had mentioned many things about my private life. As you were all strangers to me I was quite satisfied it was genuine. His reply was, "That doesn't matter. Can't you see that the medium is a thought reader and reads your subconscious mind?" Well, tonight my husband related several matters that could not possibly be in my subconscious mind, as I knew nothing about them. If Mr Walsh can not only read what is in my subconscious, but also tell me things that are NOT in it, then he is wasting his time here. He could make a fortune on the stage as the greatest thought reader that ever was. In fact I would think that kind of thought reading harder to believe than the simple fact that he is a direct voice medium!'

September 1933: There were twelve sitters at this meeting. While we were singing, the voices of many children were heard all around the room —direct spirit voices, independent of the trumpet. They said they had been allowed to come down to the room to play with us. We heard soft, childish laughter and little hands clapping. We felt the little hands tapping us on our shoulders and on our heads. Tiny fingers tugged at the end of sleeves or trousers, or tried to pull off some of the ladies' shoes. I felt one little hand untie my shoelace. Some felt the little fingers caressing their faces and gently pulling their hair. We could actually SEE these spirit hands as they moved around the room, sometimes right up near the ceiling, flickering here and there like little birds.

One of the women lifted one foot and gaily called upon the spirit children to try and pull off her shoe—which they did.

It was like an animated, spiritual kindergarten. The children's voices and fingers were everywhere; carrying and strumming the guitar all around the room; placing the luminous crucifix gently into the hands of each sitter; whisking the trumpet with amazing speed from one end of the room to the other, tapping it on some of our heads, tapping the ceiling and twirling it around the light shade—then you would hear a childish voice saying, 'I love playing with the twumpet!' They brought into the room an atmosphere of pure joy which it is impossible to describe.

May 1934: Betty, one of the spirit children, asked us to bring along coloured beads—'lots and lots of them, and plenty of string'. At the next meeting many coloured beads were placed on the floor. When the spiritual power was sufficiently built up, we began to see little hands appear. We heard the clicking of beads and childish voices laughing and talking. When the lights went up we saw on the floor all sorts of small articles made with the beads—tiny canoes, baskets, little men and animals! I have two of these bead ornaments in my possession still.

October 1935: At a trumpet meeting held at Madame Gisel's home, a Mrs Ada Hunter was invited. She looked very much like a pocket edition of the late Sophie Tucker, complete with gravel voice and infectious laugh.

During the night a man's voice spoke to her through the trumpet. She gave a gasp of astonishment. 'Don't be afraid, my dear. I am James Wilson. I was your mother's first husband'.

'James Wilson? Good gracious, so you are! How—how are you?'

'I am very well, and I have brought someone else along, too.'

Then a woman's voice was heard saying, 'Ada, it's your sister, Elsie'.

Another gasp from Ada. 'Elsie! Why you died when you were eighteen months old!' 'I know, my dear. But I have grown up'.

That was Mrs Hunter's first introduction to Walsh's trumpet meetings.

Her warm personality brought very bright conditions into the room. She and Hetty had many witty arguments which aroused gales of laughter from members.

February 1936: Mrs Hunter was invited for the first time to Mrs May's home in North Melbourne. The Mays were theatrical folk. Monty was for years a chorus man in the J. C. Williamson musical comedies and finished up as permanent wardrobe man. His wife was wardrobe mistress, a genial, plump little woman who always looked as if she was making her third curtain call before a large and enthusiastic audience. She and Mrs Hunter soon became firm friends.

One night Mrs May said to Walsh, 'Do you think we could spread this bunch of carnations on the floor? The children might like to play with them?' Said Walsh, 'By all means'.

Peter, one of the spirit children held some of the flowers to the noses of some of the sitters to smell. Mrs Hunter said, 'Peter, I wish you would put some of them on my lap'.

'All right, Mrs Hunter', piped up Peter, 'I'll put your favourite flowers on your lap'.

After the meeting she found a bunch of roses on her knees.

'Good gracious, Peter HAS given me my favourites—roses! But they were not on the floor. He must have brought them into the room!'

Hetty suddenly appeared through Walsh and lisped: 'I thay, Ada, old girl. Look at the vath on the piano. That'th where Peter got them from'. The vase was on the piano all right—minus the roses.

April 1936: Mrs Sherburne came along one Sunday night. She had the gift of automatic writing, and many poems were written through her by an unseen hand. Up to then she was unable to find the name of their author. She brought the book of poems along with her, and asked permission to place it on the floor.

During the night she heard a voice say to her through the trumpet: 'My name is Stevenson, and I am using your hand for writing. I have left a little message for you in your book'.

After the meeting she found the following message written on the open page: 'I will always help you in your work. I have been sent from God to you. God bless you and keep you in his sight. Watch, pray and love. R.L.S.'

A curious sequel was related to me by her some weeks after. One day when passing a second-hand bookshop she suddenly felt impelled to go inside. When she did she saw on one of the shelves, among a stack of second-hand books, one with the title: A Life of R. L. Stevenson. Seeing that she could have it for the princely sum of one shilling, she bought it. When she got it home, she found a copy of one of Stevenson's letters on one of the pages. She compared it with the message written in the spirit hand and was impressed by the resemblance. Reproductions of this spirit letter and the letter in the book are retained in my collection of evidential matter and items from these days. The Sherburne family have the originals.

July 1936: Professor Gunn from the Melbourne University asked if he could come along. He came to Mrs May's home. On the first night he attended there were many visitors, including three or four, who, like the Professor, had never been before. The conditions were not good. The trumpet flew around; several voices spoke to some present and a trance lecture was given; but nothing came through the trumpet of an evidential nature. It was a disappointing night.

After the meeting Walsh said to the Professor, 'I'm sorry you didn't get a message, but conditions were not very good tonight'.

Professor Gunn, who was a rather young man, replied, 'As a matter of fact I was very interested in the lecture on spirit phenomena and how it operates on the other side. As for absence of any evidential phenomena, that lack convinced me more than if there had been a profusion of incidents. After all, if you were a charlatan, you would have made quite sure that sufficient phenomena were forthcoming to suit all parties'.

This was a very sensible reply from a very sensible man. He came again the following week when results were more satisfactory. He took notes of several incidents and was satisfied that everything was genuine. He said the reason for his visits was purely psychological; he was interested in all phases of the human mind, whether normal or paranormal. This was his first experience of paranormal events and he admitted, quite frankly, that he didn't know what to make of it. Nevertheless, he was quite convinced in his own mind of the integrity and sincerity of Walsh's mediumship.

He came for several more nights and recorded quite a lot in his notebook. On the last night he told Walsh that what he had seen during these nights had been well worthwhile and would give him thought for some considerable time.

August 1934: I met Bert and Stan in town one night. We were going to a show at Her Majesty's Theatre. They looked as it they had something on their minds, so I asked them what was the matter.

'Well, it's like this', began Bert...

'Perhaps I had better explain', interrupted Stan. He gave me one of his warm smiles and said, 'Les, Mrs McIntosh wants to bring her husband, Arch, to the circle. He has been told all about the séances, but he has also heard that you were once a professional ventriloquist. He claims—now don't laugh—that you throw your voice into the trumpet and imitate all the different spirit voices heard. Now, would you mind very much if you were asked not to come to the trumpet séance next Thursday? That's the night he will be coming'.

I grinned at them. 'I don't mind at all if it will convince him'. So I stayed away that night. I had met Arch McIntosh on an earlier occasion. He was a big man with a bright manner, and a great infectious laugh. I could quite understand his desire to come along and see for himself whether or not the reports of the meetings were true. He was plainly sceptical and I could appreciate his suspicions about my ventriloquial powers. He was an honest sceptic and I admired his honesty. He no doubt voiced the suspicions of plenty of others who had not bothered to come along and find out the truth for themselves.

Later, I heard that the night had been a great success. Many spirit voices spoke through the trumpet and Arch himself, received a message that was evidential. I met him a week or so later and he told me he was sorry he suspected me. 'I can see I was rather stupid to think it was ventriloquism, but apart from that, the long message I received from my mother convinced me beyond any doubt. Even if you had been there you could not have said what she said, because she spoke to me of intimate problems that you couldn't have possibly known'.

Arch didn't come very often. He was a busy man. His admiration for Walsh, whom he used to refer to, humourously, as the 'Messiah', was unbounded. 'No one else but the 'Messiah' could have convinced me about the afterlife', he once said to me.

During those years many hundreds of people came by invitation to those meetings and some amazing evidential messages were given. I cannot recall one instance where these visitors were not satisfied with what they heard and experienced at the direct voice gatherings. But I do recall numerous times when their delight was boundless. One could never assess the amount of comfort given through contact with relatives who now live in peace and happiness in the world of spirit.

However, one must not count the satisfaction of curiosity, simple delight, or even the comfort given, as the most important end result of the spiritual work of these years of direct voice sessions. Their primary purpose was to prove to a misguided world the certainty of Eternity.

The aluminium trumpet, or megaphone, kept for Mrs Martin's direct voice meetings, which brought through the voices of so many who once lived on this earth plane—people from every walk of life and belonging to every creed and belief—is now safely tucked away in my study; but it is a memento only now. When Stan Walsh died, the trumpet power that he possessed died with him.

20

LUMINOSITY

> The world is in a welter of the possible and impossible, and no one knows what will be the next scientific hypothesis to confirm some ancient miracle.
>
> G. K. CHESTERTON

As previously stated, many outsiders who heard of the biblical personalities who controlled Walsh, used to say: 'What proof is there that they are really Saints of the Bible?' Apart from their extraordinary wisdom—'no man spake like this man'—the greatest proof of their authenticity was the dramatic gift of 'luminosity' given to Walsh, a spectacle that I do not think has been witnessed since Biblical times.

There is a continuous stream of references in both the Old and New Testament regarding these 'Lights' or 'Transfigurations'. This gift, declared the High Guides, came directly from Christ, Himself, the 'Light of the World'. Everyone privileged to see these luminous sights agreed that literally, they had to be seen to be believed.

The first historical (Biblical) mention of supernatural Light made visible to the human eye is in Exodus, Chapter 14, where it states that there stood between the camp of the Israelites and the army of the Egyptians a pillar of cloud by day and a pillar of fire by night.

Again in Exodus, Chapter 34, Verse 29 onwards, it is recorded that when Moses came down from Mount Sinai with the Ten Commandments he did not realise that Light shone from his face. When Aaron and the Elders saw the Light shining they were afraid—so Moses put a veil over his face when he spoke to them.

There are many other references—more so in the New Testament than the Old, but the most famous one is where Jesus was transfigured on a high mountain before his disciples. It says in Matthew, Chapter 17, Verses 2 onwards: 'And He was transfigured before them, and His face did shine as the sun, and His raiment was white as Light'.

In exactly the same manner, and with many variations, was the Light shown through Walsh. It often shone from his face, indeed, on occasions, 'his raiment was as white as Light'.

During the last few years of Walsh's life this gift was developed to such an extent that nearly all who came along to his various meeting nights were able to witness, along with his regular followers, the amazing spectacle of these transfigurations.

'By their fruits you shall know them'. Through this revealing gift, everyone—and there were hundreds of witnesses over the years—KNEW without a shadow of doubt, that the Biblical characters these High Guides purported to be, were, in fact, in their presence.

Such a gift could only come from the 'secret places of the most high', which, we had explained to us, is the Eleventh Plane of Light in the spirit world—the highest plane of all and nearest to Almighty God Himself or 'The Absolute' or 'Divine Source of All' or whatever name one may choose.

This gift of luminosity was first developed in Walsh within the Inner Circle. When it was perfected there it began to appear in the other séance rooms.

One Tuesday night we were told that the High Guides were working upon the body of the instrument to enable this gift to be developed. It took many months before it was finally developed and entailed a lot of suffering for Walsh.

We did not know, at the time, that he was to become a human lamp or torch. We were told that this spiritual light which was to come down from the 'most high' was too dazzling to be revealed in its actual spiritual state, so Walsh's body had to be worked upon in such a manner that he would become, what we call nowadays a 'transformer'. The brilliant light passing through this human power house would be 'dimmed' or 'broken down' when it materialized so that it could be seen by human eyes without too much strain on human eyesight.

Walsh was told to have no fear. He would not be harmed, and the pain would eventually go. No doubt to comfort our human minds, we were told that qualified medical doctors who had passed into the spirit world and had risen high, were co-operating with the High Guides, to bring about the physical changes necessary in the medium's body to enable the light to shine through, in its reduced state. It was an added lesson to us to realize that the skills and talents we develop in our human lives are ours forever.

It is necessary to state that this pain was not forced upon Walsh. As he grew older he became more and more a man of prayer. He prayed, always, for the highest and was always prepared to pay for the highest. If part of the payment meant 'pain', he was prepared to honour the debt. He could withdraw from the obligation set before him by these High Guides, if he wanted to but he chose not to withdraw. Of his own free will he accepted what was offered to him, even though there were thorns attached to the gift.

Some months after this announcement, we three went for our usual annual holiday together to Sydney, staying at the home of Jones' old friends, Mr and Mrs Goldsmith in Queenscliffe, New South Wales. During these three weeks Jones and I spent much time in the surf during the day. Walsh spent most of the time on the sofa—in pain. Sometimes the pain would be bad, at other times a lot easier.

When we came back to Melbourne he was too ill to hold meetings. His family persuaded him to see their family doctor, a Dr Drew. To please them, he did. Said the Doctor: 'It's about time you gave up this trance business'. He had heard about it. He finally advised him to at least rest in the hills.

'But I've just returned from a holiday', said Walsh.

'Well you can't go back to work yet'.

So Walsh went up to Kallista in the Dandenongs with his family. Jones and I visited him there on weekends. Two weeks later he came home, feeling much better. During a social call to Mrs Martin, Malocca suddenly interrupted the conversation by taking over Walsh's body and said: 'My "Black-eye" (the name he called his charge) will be alright from now on. High Guides finish their work. Him be all right from now on. You tell him'. We did.

A week later he felt so much better that he decided for his family's sake to pay another visit to Dr Drew, to have his return to good health confirmed. He told the Doctor he felt quite well again and would like to start work the next day. 'But I wanted to arrange an X-ray for you' said the Doctor. 'I'm all right now. I'm sure it's not necessary', said Walsh. The Doctor shook his head, 'you're a strange fellow', was the rejoinder. 'Anyhow, be sure to come back if there is any more pain'.

The next week Walsh said he felt well enough to start the Inner Circle again. The other meetings would follow later. For about a month after that only the Inner Circle meeting was held, and it was during that time that the first Light was revealed! His gift of luminosity had been successfully developed in him by the High Guides and their helpers.

While we need have no doubt that God could have used miraculous means to 'instantly' dispose this gift of luminosity on the medium—who had voluntarily surrendered his body to the purposes of God through prayer—the process used was in accordance with our rate of progress, and in complete obedience to those physical laws which human minds could understand. We should be able to 'take the point' of this example. God obviously does not want our grasp of spiritual knowledge to run wildly ahead of our knowledge of the physical laws of our universe—nor the reverse, as man entering his 'space age' would seemingly have it. Spiritual science and physical science are really one and the same, and our knowledge, and application of knowledge to our own development, should run parallel in each field of understanding.

There were many lessons for us to take from this 'slow-motion' induction of a great gift to a humble recipient. Many of us are chosen to suffer in life. There has to be a reason, whether we come to fully understand it in this life or not, but the thing that we can look for, and pray about is the 'hidden gift'—hidden, that is, until we willingly discover it. It may not be a gift or a blessing as spectacular as Walsh's gift of luminosity, but to our lives and the lives of those who come within the span of our influence, we may find it almost as far-reaching.

For Stan Walsh and his followers, who had been instructed especially to call themselves 'Followers of the Truth of God', this gift of luminosity had particular significance. As Lowell said: 'Light is the symbol of Truth'.

The first indication of what was to follow, came one Tuesday night. John the Most Beloved was giving us one of his heart warming talks concerning the little known private life of Christ on earth. As His closest friend he had much to tell us.

During this conversation he said that Christ was very close to us, even as he was speaking. A new power had been brought down into the room by His presence, and this could and would be shown to us before the night was over.

A little later, after John had left the Medium's body, we saw something beginning to shine in the centre of the floor. At first it looked like a daub of light about the size of a saucer. We kept on watching it, as we were singing, then it gradually formed into a cross of light about five or six inches long. We stopped singing and excitedly knelt down on the floor to examine it. It stayed there for the rest of the evening, gradually fading away just before we closed the service.

Malocca explained that this was the forerunner of the gift of Light brought down to us by the power of Christ, working through the High Guides present in the room. Naturally we were greatly excited by this new development, and looked forward eagerly to the next Tuesday night.

This time, to our astonishment, the Light appeared on the right lapel of each of the white robes which we always wore at Inner Circle meetings— and gradually formed into small crosses. They shone for most of the night, but slowly faded away before the close of the meeting.

On the third Tuesday night after the promise, Vashti, who was controlling Walsh, took hold of Mabel Grenville's hand and mine, and, at the same time, stood Walsh upon his feet. Still holding our hands he raised Walsh's until they were straight in front of him. He then released our hands and brought the medium's hands together as if in prayer. I must emphasise the fact that we held both the medium's hands in ours, until a few seconds before Walsh's hands were brought together held straight in front of him—then, without warning, a thin bright Light, like a searchlight, shone out from between the palms of his hands.

It lit up the whole room and we could see each other clearly. Vashti then began to walk around the room sending the Light in every direction. It rested for a while on the picture of Christ, so that every small detail of the portrait, which had been painted under trance, could be seen. As he walked slowly around he began to speak to us:

> Friends, this is the Light of God sent to you, and made visible before your eyes. It has been made possible by the great faith of each one of you. But remember that this Light has been sent for a specific purpose. It is sent by God, in the name of Christ, through this man, that it might shine OUT BEYOND the room and into the darkened souls of many in the world. This Light, each time it shines—and it will do so in many forms—will be the means of saving many whom you will never meet or see on earth.

It is sent out, not only to those who feel they are in darkness or have lost their way on earth, but also to many who dwell in darkness in the spirit world.

Great darkness will envelop this earth in the near future. Evil men in authority in other lands, even now, are planning to crush and control the freedom of many. This good man and other worthy vessels throughout the world, have been chosen by God to see that the world is not enslaved by these evil rulers. This man's task is to send out that Light. Although disaster comes to the earth and evil forces will be let loose, they will not prevail. The Light will eventually drive out the darkness. It will inspire men and women of freedom loving countries to fight these forces of evil and darkness, and save the world from slavery and utter degradation.

Vashti, of course, was referring to the Second World War, which came a long time after this prophecy.

From then onward the Light developed in many ways. It shone not only through Walsh, but passed from him into many who were present at these meetings. When meetings for other nights were resumed, the Light that had developed in the Inner Circle, began to appear at these other meetings. Even though this was only the first stage of Walsh's gift of luminosity, it was so extraordinary to ordinary human reasoning that when the news spread abroad that an unexplainable Light shone through the hands of the medium, it was proposed that he was concealing a small torch.

While to us this suggestion was too absurd to be taken seriously, it was only fair to those, whose scepticism was honest, to refute these arguments to the best of our ability. Assuming that people will be convinced by the weight of evidence, we were quick to point out that each time the Light shone, two different sitters would take the responsibility of holding the medium's hands for a few seconds before the phenomenon occurred in order to give the necessary 'strength' to the instrument to bring the Light through. For Walsh to have a small torch or globe in his hands would have been quite impossible, unless the whole complement of the meeting was involved in trickery.

As if to assist us in convincing others of the honesty of these occasions, Vashti, one night, parted the instrument's hands while the Light was still shining. There was the Light shining through the tips of each finger—and hands wide open!

We had hardly recovered from this when a further advancement was made within the Inner Circle. One night, during the singing, Malocca jumped the instrument to his feet, opened his mouth wide and a long sliver of white fire darted from the medium's mouth! Breathing hard, Malocca walked around the room and shone this fire-like Light on the face of each sitter. We were speechless! As time went on, the Light began to spread all over the medium's body. Many of the guides, as they controlled him, showed their spiritual robes of Light draped on the body of the instrument. On these special occasions, with the Light shining from his face and his hands and his body draped in a robe of Light, he was literally transfigured.

One night, at Bert Jones' home, Wagga, Mrs Beames' Indian guide controlled Walsh. In deep guttural tones he described how, as a Red Indian chief, he had dwelt in the forests of North America. He described a tribal war between his tribe and an enemy tribe.

As he spoke the body of the instrument began to slowly light up, the brilliant light gradually spreading from the head to the feet. We began to discern the outline of a robe of Light, and on his head the outline of a huge Indian head-dress of feathers—all in Light. The whole of Walsh's face was transformed by Light. He walked around the room, with arms folded, in typical Red Indian fashion, shining brightly. Tucked underneath the arms were the ends of the robe with a long fringe of Light, hanging gracefully over the folded arm.

The deportment and majestic bearing of this imposing Chief—all in Light—had to be seen to be appreciated. It was a breath-taking experience.

Although Wagga's story was told in broken English, it was full of poetic images, and rendered with extraordinary dramatic power. He finished by saying that he had been sent by the power of God to bring the Light of the Son of the Great White Spirit (meaning Jesus Christ) down into the room. The materialisation of his robe in Light was shown as a visible sign of the Power. Many outside the room, that night, in this city, in this land and shining even to distant lands, he added, would benefit by that Light.

During one of John the Most Beloved's many visits to us, he spoke again of the Second Coming of Christ. As he spoke the medium was transfigured in a garment of Light, resembling the type of white robe used in Biblical times. He said that the Robe of Light was witness to the near presence of Christ to the room.

He also repeated what other High Guides had said, that the Light was not shown purely for our satisfaction, or for idle curiosity. It was sent through the instrument to shine out into the world to guide the return of the 'lost' in many countries, to comfort the bereaved and to help those in distress. He said that Walsh was used as a human lamp of God. If this pure Light was sent directly from God to those in need of help, they would not feel, or, at least they would not comprehend it. But when the Light passes through a human body, or is given human strength, combined with the Divine Power, it is then able to penetrate into the minds and souls of all who need God's love. To demonstrate what he meant, he asked Mabel Grenville to stand up. He took her two hands and asked us to pray with him that the Light would shine through Mabel's body. He turned Mabel round so that her back faced us. In a few minutes we could distinctly see a Light penetrating her gown and covering the whole of her back. Slowly it formed into a large cross which stretched from her shoulders down to the edge of her gown. The cross of Light was so strong that it lit up the whole room.

'Thus you see how the Light of God can shine through', he concluded, 'and is revealed to you that you might believe and understand'.

Again at Mrs Martin's home, a Hindu priest who had lived in Pasha, in India, seventeen hundred years ago, spoke to us. He lectured on the power of Thought. As he talked his spiritual robe slowly materialised in Light. As he finished his talk he asked us to touch it gently. On examination it appeared to be made of intricate lacy patterns, exquisite in design. It felt like soft, silvery gauze or gossamer—it is very difficult to give an accurate description of what it really was like. For instance, when the meeting was over, a fine silvery substance, like quicksilver, was strewn on the floor, the remains of the partly materialised gown.

Following the night when the cross of Light was shown on Mabel's back, this same lighted cross began to appear on the robes of other sitters. Many guides began to come through, robed in Light, or wearing their national costumes, worn by them on earth, in Light. One of them was Marshal Ney of Napoleon's army who came through, and confirmed the prophecies of other guides of the coming of a Second World War. A war which would be the most disastrous in the history of the world. Many nations would be overrun and fall including his own country—France—but the latter, he added, would rise again. As he spoke his uniform slowly built up in Light— one could even see the lighted epaulettes on his shoulders.

These transfigurations continued for over two years of various types of guides who came through lit up in the robes, or native costumes, they wore on earth. They were a source of wonder and inspiration to all that witnessed them.

One night the Hindu seer, Armah Singh, asked us to bring along a crystal ball. Mrs McIntosh brought one to the next meeting. In due course came Armah Singh who took the ball and, while seated, held it on his knees. Slowly the ball lit up and in it were shown symbols, figures and pictures—which we were all able to see.

Only clairvoyants can look into a crystal ball and see what is revealed in it, but when the Light shone through the ball held by the seer one did not need to be clairvoyant to see what was there. After that, if a ball was not available, the Sadhu would ask for a glass jug full of water, or a glass salad bowl, for the same purpose—that is, the Light would shine through them also, showing what the guides wished us to see.

One night the ball was lit up as usual and the Sadhu called me over to look into it. He said: 'Friend, look into the ball, and there you will see your Indian Guide, Red Chief. As I looked into it I could see, quite clearly, a tall Red Indian chief, with a strong, lean face, a beautiful headdress of 98 coloured leathers, arms folded, looking at me. It was a wonderful experience. Many others saw their guides in the same manner.

Many who were sick were brought to the meetings to be healed by this Light shining through the instrument's hands. Often, there was absent healing also. In such cases a guide would come through and ask all to join hands. Then a prayer would be given for the sick. We would give the names of the sick, especially those absent from the meeting and then we would include others that we did not know by name. As we prayed and concentrated with the guide, the Light would again shine through Walsh's hands and light up the whole room.

On another night, Sunday, when there were many visitors, Sadhu asked each one to come forward and look into the ball, one at a time. As they did a beautiful woman could be seen in a pure white robe edged with gold. She was surrounded by the spirits of young women, all robed in various colours. 'The one in the centre', he said, 'is Mary Magdalene. The others around her are spirit helpers. They are young women who left the earth plane years ago and have risen high. Mary Magdalene is their leader. They have come down to take the strength of your human prayers to especially help young women everywhere. The faith of human minds, combined with the divine power of God brought down by these very highly developed souls, enables them to perform miracles in the hearts of many young women who need help, and in young womanhood in general whose values and strength are important both in these times and in the future'.

I recall one night when I had a throat infection. My throat was so badly inflamed I could hardly swallow. I hesitated as to whether I should go to the usual sitting of the Inner Circle, but I did not like missing the meeting, so I set off wrapped up in a heavy overcoat and thick woollen scarf. My throat was so bad that I could not sing. Later Red Chief came through and immediately the Light began to shine through the medium's hands. He came over to me and shone the Light all around my throat, while the others sang. Before the meeting closed I realised, to my astonishment, that the inflammation of the throat had completely gone. I sang the last hymn with the rest of them with not a vestige of soreness left.

Here is an extract from a letter I received from one of the regular sitters at Madame Gisel's home. She wrote:

> 'My friend, Mrs Caplan, asked Mr Walsh if I could come along to one of his meetings. He consented. When I arrived there I was very nervous as I was a stranger to everyone in the room, and had never been to any meetings or séances before. After half an hour or so, seeing and hearing spirit phenomena I heard my Christian name called. Mr Jones took me by the hand and led me up to Mr Walsh, who was sitting down under deep trance. A crystal ball was in his hands, all lit up, and the guide asked me to look into it. I did so, and these were the words I saw written in long hand inside the bowl: "George loves you!" George was my late husband. I was overjoyed.
>
> Later, he spoke to me through the trumpet, but I shall never forget those words written in the crystal ball.'

One night Armah Singh held the lighted crystal ball in his hands and prophesied the Second World War. As he held it he said, 'Within the crystal ball are the flags of all the nations who will be Allies of Britain, including Russia'. He then invited each sitter to walk over and look in the ball.

One sitter, on seeing the Australian flag there, asked, 'What about Australia?' The Seer replied, 'The war will come very close to this country. There will be a threat of invasion from the North, but your country will be safe.'

Apropos of the prophecy that Russia would be one of our Allies, I remember, much later, when the war did come that I met one of the sitters who had been at the séance, and he said, 'I see Russia has signed a pact with Germany, and yet, according to Armah Singh, she was supposed to be one of our Allies!' I couldn't answer that one, but later, the seer was justified in his prophecy. Russia, as we all know, was unexpectedly invaded by Germany, and, overnight, came over to the Allies!

The Guides were never far from us, no matter where we went, turning up at the most unexpected times. The last time we visited Sydney together was in December, 1938. On New Year's Eve the Goldsmiths held a party at their house. In the midst of one of the dances Walsh disappeared from the big dining room. Jones went to look for him. A few minutes later he returned and beckoned me. I followed him into the bedroom.

'Vashti has controlled Stan,' he said. When we entered the room there he was sitting on the bed, under control. In his hand he held a plain glass marble, the type that was used in lemonade bottles years ago.

It was lit up. We were told to look into the marble. Right inside it could be seen a tiny miniature of Christ, sideways on, and looking up, while the Light of God shone down on to His face. He was robed in white with a red shoulder cloak. Vashti said: 'This is to let you see Jesus the Christ, even now, praying to God that the Light from Him will shine even brighter in the New Year into your world, which will soon be drawn into great darkness!'

Outside could be heard the noise of dancing, music and laughter. Someone started to play the Lambeth Walk. We left the room shortly afterwards and returned to the dance. A few months later the world was plunged into the greatest disaster of all time, World War II.

There was an occasion when something occurred which was, perhaps, even more extraordinary than those already recounted about this unpredictable Light. One night at Mrs Martin's home, Malocca said that the Light of God would be seen that night shining through the medium's heart! It was a very hot night and we men had all shed our coats. Walsh wore a light open necked shirt. Later, as we were singing Malocca suddenly appeared and said: 'Look!' A great red Light shone out from the medium's chest and, looking into it, we could see his heart, quite plainly, contracting and expanding in a steady beat!

It was like looking into a brightly illuminated X-ray picture in vivid red. We could see every vein and muscle around the heart. The Light seemed to shine through the heart, capturing the colour of the blood vessels. It was a strange, uncanny sight to see each sitter come forward, at Malocca's bidding, and look with astonishment into the steadily beating heart. One of the sitters said afterwards, speaking for us all, 'What will happen next? If we were to tell anyone outside what had happened they would say we are mad, or dreaming!'

This happened! When I told a member of our Thursday meetings, George Allum, what had happened at our Sunday night meeting he was incredulous. George, once an honest sceptic, had eventually become a regular Thursday night member. He was now deeply impressed by the evidential nature of what he saw and heard; nevertheless he found it hard to understand how a human heart could be lit up, as described.

'So do we find it hard to understand George, but wait and see for yourself,' I said. George had to wait a few weeks before anything like that happened again. It is not possible to switch on to any particular psychic phase or phenomena at a moment's notice.

One Friday night George Allum invited us to his home at Ascot Vale, together with other members of the Thursday circle. I was secretly hoping that the Light would shine through Walsh's heart during that meeting, but it didn't. After supper, we made ready for home. We walked slowly out of the front door, and strolled into the street with George and his wife. Combined moonlight, and the bright light of a near-by street lamp almost turned night into day. Without warning, there was a breathless gasp from Walsh as Malocca controlled him, and, there in the lighted street, a red light shone out from the instrument's chest. Malocca had quickly pulled back the medium's coat and revealed his white shirt underneath. George and his wife stared in astonishment at the red light, the beating heart with the veins and muscles around it pulsating rhythmically. When Walsh came to and asked what had happened, we told him. George and his wife were dumbfounded. To say that he was convinced is a slight understatement.

Just one more description of an unusual variation of the Light phenomena: Professor Jenkinson said in a lecture that all masterpieces in art, music, sculpture, painting and literature came to man from God. As he spoke of this I remembered reading in the lives of Haydn and Beethoven, that the former, when receiving an ovation for one of his compositions, pointed upwards and said, 'It came from above', and the latter, when praised by admirers for one of his great works, said, 'It was given to me'. The Professor explained, 'Great works are already waiting in the Kingdom of God, to be brought down by hard working, sincere, naturally gifted painters, writers, sculptors, poets and composers and others.'

To illustrate this point the Professor said he had brought a book that had been 'prepared' on the other side. Its important contents had not yet been given to this world through the brain of a man, but it would be presented thus someday, when the right man was chosen—one worthy of the gift. As he spoke the light began to shine through Walsh's hands and, very slowly, a book was semi-materialized in Light. It could be clearly seen by all in the room resting on the medium's hands. The Professor then stood Walsh up and asked each of us to place our hands, palms upwards, on our knees. He then took the *book of Light* and, approaching each of us in turn, placed it gently on the open palms of our hands and as it rested there slowly turned over the leaves of this illustrated book.

It felt soft and downy to the touch. Dim pictures and printing could be seen on each page of *Light*, but not clearly enough for discernment. After showing it to each one, he said: 'This is a book yet to be presented on the earth plane. It will arrive when the time is right. The inspiration for it is conceived in the spirit world and will be brought down in due time to the mind of the man or woman chosen for the task of writing it. God plans happiness for us in many ways, and one of the ways through which this is accomplished is through cultural channels. This is just one of the many gifts in store for mankind, one that will bring pleasure to thousands'.

21

INSPIRATION

> Inspirations that we deem our own are our divine foreshadowing and foreseeing of things beyond our reason and control
>
> LONGFELLOW

Professor Jenkinson, whom the reader has already met in the chapter on automatic painting and materialization of colour was chosen to instruct us on the subject of inspiration. His lectures were in themselves an inspiration.

When men of genius, or specialists in their particular vocation, such as scientists, painters, writers, composers, inventors, accountants and statesmen, go back to the spirit world, they eventually gravitate to that area of their spiritual plane where there are gathered many other souls interested in that particular field. Like is drawn to like. That law persists in the spirit world as well as in the physical world.

When a great painter dies he goes, eventually, to the particular sphere where there are other painters. If he is a composer, he is irresistibly drawn to all other musicians and composers in the musical sphere—all writers to the writing sphere, and so on.

Each have their particular sphere in the world of spirit. One could liken this to the earthly associations, such as the Royal Academy of Art, the Medical Association, Musical Association, Institutes of Scientists., etc.

Every now and then a child is born with a gift of some kind. When God wills it, a spark of Light from one of the above spheres goes to the earth to inhabit a new human life. Such a child is recognised, in a very short time, as 'gifted' or 'talented'.

A child may be born with the gift of painting. As he develops he finds it easy to sketch or draw—then he begins to be influenced by those souls from the painting sphere who become his spiritual patrons. They urge him, in thought, to study and work hard. If the chosen person responds to the pressure of the thoughts of these gifted souls in spirit, he finds himself driven, and knows not how or why. He finds a constant inward urge to work, to study, to fiercely concentrate on painting, and even at times, to give up everything for the sake of Art.

He, or she, to a certain extent, is 'possessed' by the Divine Influence through these great souls from the painting sphere. The exalted force and vibration of these great masters of Art fill the earthly subject with a great longing to give of their best—to respond to God's great love for them through their Art.

The old saying that 'genius' is ninety-nine per cent perspiration and one per cent inspiration, is true. But it is also true that the fanatical urge to work hard is prompted by the inspiration of these exalted beings in spirit. It is in fact through inspired perspiration that the mind of a dedicated person is overwhelmed by that one per cent inspiration that comes from above. There is only one magnet that can draw down inspiration from on high and that is hard work and sustained concentration.

The harder a person works at his paintings, writings, scientific experiments, or strives to solve some complicated business problem, or tries to build up successful organisations for the uplift of the fallen or downtrodden, or assist in the alleviation of the suffering — anything where man's true motive is for the benefit or improvement or happiness of his fellow men—such a man, by his courage, his will to win, and his refusal to accept defeat draws down the inspirational help of these great souls who once specialised in what he is doing.

All those souls of once great people from the past who visited our meetings in spirit acknowledged that their greatness had come not FROM them, but THROUGH them. They were instruments. All cultural, social and altruistic achievements are FIRST conceived in spirit, and brought down through them because they invited the inspiration of the spirits by their attitude.

All that is needed is to find a young man or woman with the necessary gift and capacity for hard work, and in due time, the success that they desire will come—with the aid of exalted spiritual beings, working through them to that end.

The professor, and other guides, were anxious, however, to point out that inspiration or spiritual guidance, was not only for professional men or women in top positions or top ranking cultural exponents, but also for the ordinary man or woman in the street.

St Teresa of Avila, the Catholic saint, was right when she said that 'angels are to be found among the pots and pans in the kitchen, as well as in the Church'. The guides confirmed this truth when they taught that our personal, hidden guide and friend—our Guardian Angel—is also with us in the factory, the office, the home, the school and the playing fields. Everywhere you go your guide goes too.

Professor Jenkinson added that the advice given to us by our guides, usually via our subconscious mind, is not only wise and true, but is full of downright common sense.

Guardian angels are forthright, loving, realistic and completely practical—that is, where it is necessary to help us solve very real and down-to-earth problems. An angelic being is always a super-intelligent being.

22

A PROPHET OF MODERN TIMES

> The Lord shall raise up unto thee a Prophet, from the midst of thee, of thy brethren
>
> DEUTERONOMY 18:15

Walsh was the perfect example of a Prophet of Modern Times. Over the years he had been prepared and developed in such a way as to allow the High Guides of God to come down and proclaim by word and by signs, the Second Advent of Christ.

Those who spoke of this Second Coming were: John the Baptist, Daniel, John the Most Beloved, Luke the Physician, Samuel, Vashti the Egyptian Priest, the Egyptian Pharaoh, Tutankhamen, and several others.

These accounts are not able to represent the magnificent manner in which the talks were originally presented. Unfortunately tape recorders did not exist then, and we may not have been allowed to use them, anyway.

Here are some examples:

Tutankhamen: There are hidden vaults inside the pyramids which will one day be discovered. Inside these vaults will be found a stone image of the Christ, and a message carved on the walls. When translated the writings will reveal prophecies fulfilled. Tutankhamen translated one of the writings: 'When man has risen by his own power and knowledge, and in the midst of great scientific discoveries, then will come again the Christ, and His Wisdom and Light will bring a great peace to the world of Man.'

Samuel the Prophet: 'The day will come when science will put into the hands of great nations new weapons of destruction that will appal mankind. Man cannot of himself bring lasting peace to this earth. It is beyond him. Only God can bring permanent peace. There will be further wars that will bring great suffering and loss of life, but in the end the evilness that brought them about will be overcome.

Later, there will come yet another threat of a great war, but just as nations are about to rise, one against the other, with new weapons of destruction that would destroy civilization, THEN shall the Hand of God intervene. God will NOT allow this world to be destroyed. Round about this time in many lands signs will be shown by the power of God. These strange events will take place as a warning from God, and Man will wonder and fear. Then, amidst confusion and rumours of great wars, Christ will come again. Through Him shall come a lasting peace to a world which knows no peace.

Christ will sojourn on this earth for three years. He will leave behind Him disciples in every land to carry on His work after He goes back to the world of spirit. By then His task—commenced two thousand years ago— will be completed. Modern scriptures will be written and His second coming fully recorded for all time. Modern inventions will enable man to record His work and miracles throughout the world, so that these will be perpetuated, beyond doubt, in the hearts of all mankind, as God has willed.

The world will NOT come to an end when Christ comes again but the age will come to an end and future generations will find the earth a new and a far brighter and happier place to live in than it has ever been before.'

Luke the Physician: One night he came, and was transfigured in a robe of white light. He stood in our midst and, after speaking to us for a little while, began to look upward. Then he became silent, still gazing up as if watching someone. In a few moments he began to speak again, slowly, as if relaying a message. He said: 'I bring you a message from the Lord Jesus Christ. He is very close to this room. This is what

He is saying: "I shall come again, and the miracles of God shall be performed, and all mankind shall know Me".'

John the Baptist: He spoke of the Second Coming in much the same manner as the others. Someone in the room asked him if a time could be given, and John the Baptist replied: 'The time is known only to God. The Second Coming will be within the next generation or so...

Many minor prophecies were made, the most important being the coming of the Second World War. This was given many times. The first warning was given in the very early thirties. I have scribbled notes dated in the year 1931 in which this war was predicted, including the downfall of Germany. Also in the same prophecy, which was given by Armah Singh, while holding the lighted crystal ball, it was foretold that the British Empire, as we knew it then, would lose many of its possessions. When this prediction was made Armah Singh asked each one of us to come forward and look into the illuminated ball. There one could see the British Crown with every jewel stripped from it. The falling away of the jewels symbolised, he said, the loss of many of the Empire's colonies and other powerful possessions which she held at that time.

In 1928, shortly after I joined the Inner Circle, one of the guides prophesied the World Depression, in which Australia would share. He predicted that hardship and suffering would come to many, but that the members of the Inner Circle would have nothing to fear. This was fulfilled to the letter.

In the early thirties, Queen Victoria spoke to us through Walsh. 'Call me Victoria', she said, 'there are no kings or queens over here'. Among other things, she told us that her great grandson, Edward, would become King, but would not wear the crown. This prophecy puzzled us. Later, however, when his father, George V, died and he became King, followed soon after by his abdication before the official coronation, we recalled what she had said, and understood what she meant.

Marshal Ney, of France, as already recorded, spoke on one occasion. This was in 1929. He spoke, also of the coming of the Second World War, and foretold the downfall of France. 'She will come under the domination of Germany, but only for a season.'

Many prophecies foretold public events which later proved true. Among these was Japan's treacherous attack on Pearl Harbour. The tragic deaths of flyers, Sir Charles Kingsford-Smith, Amy Johnson and Bert Hinkler were also predicted with startling accuracy.

The problem with all prophecies, is the difficulty of time. Rarely do prophets give the exact time when an event will take place. In the case of spirit prophets, there is a real difficulty (for us, that is—they don't see it that way) because where they 'live' there is no time as we know it. Eternity is timeless and for us this is a hard concept to understand—for the spirits the 'difficulty' lies in comprehending our non-appreciation of a timeless Eternity.

But perhaps this inability to pinpoint an appointment with fate is just as well. Prophecies are given in order that people may find in them a direction, either to change their ways for the better, prepare adequately for some future event or see more clearly God's overall plan for His creation. They are never meant to put people into a state of panic or thrust fear in their hearts unnecessarily.

A case in point is an occasion when Vashti, the Egyptian, prophesied that in years to come a great disaster would befall one of the major cities of the world. This city, built to great height on a small island, would be destroyed by land subsidence caused by an earthquake and there would be a great loss of life brought about by the crashing down of high rise buildings. After it was over there would be a furious, world wide, public outcry demanding that high building construction for the future be limited to a reasonable height. Because of this city's important role in the affairs of all the nations of the earth the lesson would be most urgently taken.

Here students of prophecy could make a fairly accurate stab at the place, but since no time was given the element of panic-warning does not exist—although a timely warning could be taken in regard to the senseless persistence of city planners in building top-heavy metropolises as if the only way man can gain dominion of this earth plane is to head upwards!

As Carlyle once said; 'There is a BEST PATH for every man; the thing which, here and now, it were wisest for him to do'. Prophecies made for the sake of prophesying are as inadvisable as interpreting prophecies for the mere satisfaction of curiosity. On the other hand, intelligent use of the gift of prophecy is a noble and wise form of good counsel and the intelligent use of knowledge gained through prophecy is both sensible and proper.

When answering questions for personal prophecies, the spiritual guides always endeavoured to present to each enquirer, seeking advice or counsel, a vision of what they COULD do, if they tried. To bring out the best in them the guides, in the sentiment of Carlyle, tried to suggest to each enquirer the 'best path' to travel.

Here is an extract from one of John the Most Beloved's talks: 'There are two paths to travel in everyone's life. The path of our own free will, or that of God's will. If we choose the latter we must eventually find true happiness, success and peace of mind.' This was the aim of the guides in every message given under deep trance or through the direct voice amplified through the trumpet. Their first objective was to prove beyond doubt, to every sitter, earnestly seeking the Truth, that life after death was sure and certain, and that this applied to every living person of every colour, race and creed.

Their next objective was to give wise counsel about the sitter's private life, and give prophecies of what would certainly ensue IF he took their advice. Always they tried to persuade enquirers to keep in the direction which God planned them to go—even before they were born. At the same time, these guides, bearing in mind that God has given to us all the precious gift of 'free will', were careful to suggest that their listeners made their own decision, irrespective of what they, the guides, had suggested.

Many are living today in Australia, and other parts of the world whose lives are living fulfilments of prophecies given through Walsh. Theatrical folk, business and professional men and women, housewives and tradesmen make up this band. I recall a popular comedian on the Australian stage in the 'thirties. He was Cecil Kellaway. He was told that his greatest success would be in America. Later he told Walsh he could not see how that could possibly happen, because his ultimate aim was to return to England. Later, he unexpectedly received an offer to tour America. He recalled what the guide had said and accepted. He went on to become well known in television and in the motion picture world.

One other instance involved a young Greek woman, boarding at Mrs May's home. She was told at a meeting that if she took up singing lessons and worked hard at them she would, in time, become well known on Australian radio. She eventually became a very popular radio singer.

Throughout the years, I received advice and counsel from the guides that was always eminently wise, prudent and sensible. In addition I received wonderful help and advice, over and over again, in the training and rearing of my stepson, Ron. He lived with his grandparents in

South Melbourne. They would not part with him, but allowed me, as his stepfather, to train and undertake all decisions and expenses relating to his education and provide other extras which they could not afford. Later, when Ron reached eighteen years of age, he was invited to the meetings, and received advice and guidance direct from his mother, in spirit, and from the guides.

As I look back I can recall countless personal prophecies given to me, and to a host of sitters throughout the years—most of them were fulfilled. Not ALL of course, worked out. Some who came for advice failed to follow it out—the result being that events predicted did not eventuate. Here is one example: There was a young man, whom we will call Nicky. He was dark, handsome, good-natured, happy-go-lucky and had a languid air which suggested that he was suffering, secretly, from a perpetual yawn. He was a member of J. C. Williamson's male chorus, and had a very fine tenor voice.

He was told by the spirit of Enrico Caruso, the famous tenor, that he had a great singing future IF he cared to work hard. Note again, that word: 'IF'. Several messages were given to him over a period of time, all to the same purpose—he must work hard, study hard, seek out a competent teacher. He must practise for hours at a time each day, and put his heart and soul into it. If he did this he would become a great success in the concert world.

Nicky was thrilled with all this advice and encouragement. There was a great burst of energy and enthusiasm, and complete obedience to his teacher's instructions—for a season. But, Nicky was pleasure loving and lazy. Gradually he yawned himself into his original semi-comatose practice of sleeping in bed until nearly noon. He began to practise listlessly and spasmodically, never more than an hour at a time. He had a disagreement with his teacher over his failure to practise, so went to another mentor, but still dawdled his way along the beaten path of lethargic listlessness. The result was that he remained a chorus man. Then he complained that what Caruso had foretold did not come true. The fault of course was not in the prophet, but in Nicky.

On many occasions the guides would not give an indication of certain events imminent in a person's life, or even advise them. This was because in such cases it would be wrong, and not in accordance with God's will.

Here is one instance to illustrate the above: A certain accountant who attended many of the Sunday night meetings, asked, on one occasion if he could bring his father along for some private advice from the guides. At an interview, later, at Mrs Martin's home, the father was introduced to Walsh and the two sat down, alone in the sitting room. Professor Jenkinson took control and after a moment or so of silence said: 'Friend, I am unable to give you any information, for the moment. All I can see is a high wall. Could you come again?'. The old man smilingly agreed.

When Walsh came to he was told what the guide had said. He was surprised, but cheerfully agreed to see the visitor next week. But the appointment was never kept. A few days after the interview, the old man dropped dead in the street.

A problem inherent in all prophetic utterances, whether public or private, is difficulty in foretelling the exact time that an event will take place. On occasions the 'times' that were given are fairly accurate, but usually exact times were not given at all.

The simple reason as mentioned before is that there is no 'time' in the world of spirit. This makes what we call time very difficult to assess when looking into the future from the viewpoint of the spiritual beings.

When a spiritual personality, who dwells beyond space and time, looks into your life, he is, to a certain extent, in the same predicament as you are when you look back on your life. For instance: A neighbour asked me about a tall pine tree in our back yard. He said: 'When did you plant it?' I began to look back, just as a guide would look forward, and finally said: 'Well, it must be about fourteen or fifteen years ago/ But my wife, Anne, said: 'No, dear, not fifteen years ago, because I remember that the day it was planted was the day after our sixth wedding anniversary, and next month it is our twenty-fifth anniversary—so it must be nineteen years old!'

If you haven't diaries, or letters or other records to consult—or a wife who has a memory for anniversaries—estimating when an event happened in one's past life is not easy; so one can sympathise with a guide having to look uphill in time—when time is irrelevant to him anyway.

Sometimes, of course, the guides do succeed in estimating the right time, by tying up an event with something else they can see in your life, such as a birthday date or a wedding date, disclosed in the background of the event. The most important thing, of course, is that although the estimated times were often wrong, the event they prophesied did occur in due course. Here is a classical example of complete accuracy in foretelling an event, together with correct details as to how it happened, but inaccuracy in calculating the time of the event:

One night Malocca told us to warn the instrument that the factory where he worked would be burgled next Christmas Eve, which was seven or eight months ahead. He said they would break the lock on the back gate, get inside, blow open the safe and decamp with a fair amount of money.

We duly told Walsh. 'How am I going to tell the boss that?' was his reply. 'He doesn't know anything about this work, and if I tried to tell him he would think I was a crank!'

'Couldn't you say you dreamt it?' said Jones.

'I suppose so.' He did, and all he got for his pains was an incredulous snort from his boss. And when Christmas Eve came along—nothing happened!

Said Walsh: 'Are you sure Malocca said it was our factory that was to be robbed?' The answer was unanimous. 'We are sure!' And so the incident was forgotten.

Precisely one year later—right on Christmas Eve—the factory was robbed, exactly as described to the last detail!

There is a question I often had to answer, and it is one which may also occur to the reader: 'If a guide can see into the future and knows that a certain person will be a failure—as in the case of Nicky—why doesn't he tell the recipient of the message?' The aim of the guides was always to uplift, to encourage, to inspire and to bring out the highest in the lives of those to whom they gave their advice.

In the case of Nicky, they told him he would succeed IF of his own free will he did what they told him to do. If Caruso told Nicky that he would not succeed because of laziness what incentive would there have been for Nicky to try? Trying is the important thing in this life and Nicky did try—a little.

The next obvious question that may be asked is? 'If a guide knows a certain person will not heed his advice, why should he (the guide) bother to give it?'

One might ask the same question of many things in the Bible. Why did God promise the Children of Israel, after they left Egypt, that He would lead them into a land flowing with milk and honey—when He knew that generation would never see it? Why did Jesus choose Judas as one of His disciples when He must have known that he would betray Him? So the answer to the last question is: It was important that they be given a CHANCE TO TRY TO MAKE GOOD. If they did not—the choice was entirely their own.

23

HIS GREATEST FRIEND

Behold the man

JOHN: 19-5

John the Most Beloved spoke many times of his greatest Friend, Jesus of Nazareth. Referring to Jesus' birth, John pointed out that orthodox religion pictures usually show the stable at Bethlehem littered with nice, clean straw. This, however was far from the case. The real stable was indescribably filthy and evil smelling. Mary had to literally push the filth away from the manger.

During her earthly life Mary, the Mother of Jesus, was in fact, a prophetess and a medium—as indeed she has continued to be in her most exalted place on the spiritual planes. Before the three years ministry of Jesus began, regular spiritual meetings were held in their little home. Usually present were herself, Jesus, Joseph (until his death), a young man called Andrew (not the brother of Simon Peter) who was Jesus' friend of earlier days, and a few intimate friends of Mary and Joseph. At these meetings Mary would lend herself as an instrument for the spirit of God. Under deep trance, she would speak and prophesy in the name of God.

One day, when still a very young man, Jesus was working in His 'father's' work shop, and just before sundown, He suddenly saw a large white cross of Light appear on the door; a foreshadowing of what was to come, although He, at that time, did not know what it meant.

Jesus showed tremendous love for His mother. Joseph died when He was still a young man and His mother was all in all to Him. On one occasion He made a special wooden couch for her, as a present. He made it quite clear to His friends, who often visited the home, that no one was allowed to sit on it but His mother!

From young boyhood until His early twenties, Jesus and His close friend, Andrew, were as two brothers. Wherever one went, the other was to be found also. On one occasion when they were in their early teens Jesus' family left the village. Joseph had to seek work elsewhere. Andrew was very lonely without His friend. They were separated for about a year.

One day Andrew was sitting beside a river when he saw a bright light shining in front of him. He jumped up and ran as hard as he could to Jesus' former home. Just as he was about to open the door, the door was opened for him, and there stood his friend, Jesus, smiling at him.

Jesus explained that He could not find him when He came back to the village with His family, so He sent out a 'thought' for Andrew's return. When Andrew received the 'message', Jesus knew his friend was coming post haste, and opened the door, in eager anticipation, as he arrived.

It was Andrew, himself, through Walsh, who told these stories of Jesus' boyhood, and others which were not noted down. Andrew died a few years before Jesus' ministry began. He said he was called home by God to be a guide to Jesus in that ministry. The first person to meet Jesus when He died on the cross was this same Andrew, His boyhood friend, who led Him by the hand up through the planes of Light, to enter into that Light, and receive the reward from His Father in Heaven for His wonderful sacrifice.

One of the most moving talks given by John the Most Beloved was his description of the Crucifixion. He was an eye witness, as we know from the Gospels. His account was vivid and poignant.

In those days, said John, men were far more brutal and coarse than we realise. He described how two men nailed Jesus to the Cross. They did so, slowly and casually, just as if they were engaged in an ordinary carpentering job. On several occasions the big nails, which they were hammering into His hands and feet, would bend. They would then, with inhuman indifference, proceed to slowly and casually, drag out the bent nail, wrenching it from side to side with a form of iron instrument, until they were able to get it out. They would then, carefully select another nail and begin hammering again. On the Sunday night that John gave his talk, there must have been thirty people packed into Mrs Martin's dining room. When John had finished there was hardly a dry eye in the room. One night an Arab who lived in the time of Jesus came through and spoke. The name he gave was peculiar and I failed to record it at the time. One day, he said, he went to a nearby river in Palestine to bathe. As he approached the river bank he saw a man, a Jew, a little way from him, sitting near the water.

All Jews despised Arabs, and never spoke to them. To his astonishment, this Jew spoke to him, saying, 'Peace be unto you.'

'Why do you speak to me? I am an Arab.'

'Because you are my brother,' was the reply, 'all men are brothers.'

Many months later this Arab journeyed again to Palestine. As he approached Jerusalem, he saw people congregating along the wayside. As he drew close he saw that a procession was approaching. They were Roman soldiers, with some prisoners, on the way to be executed.

As he watched them go by, he recognised one of the prisoners as the stranger who had spoken to him at the river bank! He found that the man's name was Jesus of Nazareth, a carpenter. He followed the crowd, and as he witnessed the Crucifixion wept for the stranger. Later, he met some of Jesus' disciples, and became one of the early Christians.

At one meeting this description of Jesus, was given by John: He was slim of build, and of only average height. He was very quiet and unobtrusive in manner, almost to the point of shyness. He always kept Himself in the background, and was extraordinarily trustful. He clearly demonstrated that he thought the best of everyone He met. His manner was artless, simple and unaffected, but He displayed a quiet sense of humour. Although sensitive by nature, He always had a warm, friendly smile for anyone who spoke to Him.

When in a room where many were assembled, He would keep Himself well in the background. Often, He had to be pushed forward by His friends, when anyone wanted to meet Him. He was never one to speak about Himself except in relation to His Father; but loved to sit down quietly and listen to other people talking.

He was the direct mouthpiece—The Word—of God. The SECOND person of God. His teachings and sayings were not originated by Him; they came from God by DIRECT INSPIRATION. When anyone asked a question of Jesus, the power of God would come down upon him and he would be directed by the Spirit of God. That, of course, is another way of explaining the Trinity. The Second Person is the instrument of the First Person, and the Third Person the guiding force or inspirational factor. We were told that the words of God, and the answers to questions put to Jesus, were actually put onto his lips by the Spirit of God. After speaking thus under inspiration, Jesus often had no knowledge of what He had said. He spoke under not 'deep', but Divine trance.

The divine inspiration that filled Jesus was, of course, instantaneous and the Source constantly present to Him.

Jesus was a healer as well as a teacher. I recall several occasions when both John and Peter stated that Jesus healed not only those brought to Him, but those at distance who needed His healing. The healing power would leave Him and heal people far from Him—people whom He had never met. We were told that many more were healed by Jesus in this way than by direct contact healing.

Many Bible students were invited to meetings on the Sunday nights.

Then, either John or Peter would invite questions as to the sayings of Jesus.

Here are two interesting questions and answers:

QUESTION: 'Jesus said on the Cross, "My God, My God, why hast thou forsaken Me?" Did God forsake Him?'

ANSWER: 'God did not forsake Him. What Jesus actually said on the cross has been distorted by translation. He actually said: "My God, My God, why has My faith in Thee forsaken me?" This is entirely different. In His great agony, He, like all human beings in pain, found it hard to think of God through the intensity of the pain—hence the cry, more of agony, than anything else.'

QUESTION: 'In the Lord's prayer, Jesus said: "Lead us not into temptation". Does God lead us into temptation?'

ANSWER: 'Here again, the actual words have been slightly altered in translation. What Jesus really said was: "Let us not be led into temptation", which, again, gives an altogether different meaning to the sentence.'

Another important message, given by Daniel the Prophet, was to the effect that Bible students should concentrate more on the New Testament than the Old. Much of the Old Testament through countless translations and distortions, was not literally correct—more so in the passages in which it was inferred that God was cruel and vengeful. Translations of the Old Testament were first made, it must be remembered, by an ancient people who saw righteousness as being unforgiving and stern. Jesus Christ came to give us the 'good news' about God—to tell us that He was, in fact, a God of Love. Daniel directed modern Bible students to look for this message in the New Testament.

24

THE TEACHINGS OF THE GUIDES

> Teaching is more important than exhortation
>
> MARTIN LUTHER

This chapter records some of the spiritual teachings given by guides from very high planes of Light throughout the years. For twelve years I was present at most of these meetings, and these lectures were repeated many times to a variety of audiences. Some of the wisdom presented here simply underlines that which has already been recorded in previous chapters.

Here are the teachings that gives the information that was most frequently sought.

Why do so many North American Indians come to guide white people?

Thousands of Red Indians in the early years of America's history were driven from their natural habitations. When they resisted, they were killed by the white man.

They went back to the spirit world with hatred in their hearts for white people. Over and over again, however, Jesus came back to speak to them.

He pointed out that the best way to repay the white settlers for their cruelty, was to help them, and so return good for evil. That is why so many Red Indians are helping and guiding the white races.

But, there is another reason why they are chosen as guides. On earth they had a simple child-like faith in God whom they called The Great White Spirit. They lived very close to this Spirit by their simple faith and child-like obedience to His inner promptings. Often they discerned the purpose of the Great White Spirit by the process of fire. During the fire ritual, if the fire unexpectedly flared up it was regarded as an affirmative from this Spirit of what they were enquiring from him; if the fire unexpectedly died down that was regarded as a negative answer. This simple ritual was handed down from tribe to tribe, and conducted by the medicine man of each tribe.

When they sinned, their repentance was sincere and genuine. Their faith was akin to that of King David of Israel. Like him, the Red Indian trusted in God to give him strength and power in all his undertakings, great and small.

When their members died they believed that they went to the Happy Hunting Ground (our equivalent of Heaven) where the great 'Spirit' reigned supreme.

When, therefore, they returned to the spirit world—their Happy Hunting Ground—they already possessed an innate spiritual sense, or understanding, which enabled them to rise through the planes of Light very quickly. This simple, ingrained faith gave them great spiritual strength, brought about by their close proximity to the Spirit of God while on this earth. They are thus peculiarly suited to give that spiritual strength to the human beings whom they guide.

Is there any truth in the theory of Reincarnation?

No, it is not true. No one comes back to take up a life in this world more than once. When the spirit of man or woman leaves the earthly body, it is gradually purified and progresses only in the spirit world. A spirit that has sinned on earth has to cleanse itself and make atonement for its failing, only in the spirit realms. In due time it is purified and made whole, but all in the world of spirit.

No spirit comes back to the earth again in the flesh, to further its progression or purify its soul. Some, who believe that reincarnation is true, will say that they remember some of their past lives on earth. This, however, is an illusion. Their spiritual guide, at times, comes very close to them, perhaps at some critical period in their lives. The guide comes so close that he often brings into the mind of the person being guided, some knowledge of the conditions of that guide's life on earth.

These living memories of a powerful guide may be impressed so clearly on the mind of the one they are helping, that one may think he really experienced these earth conditions in his past life. As an example: He might see, in his mind's eye, the deeply wooded forests of North America.

He might feel that he is wrapped in a bearskin and almost sense a headdress of feathers on his head. This may be so vivid to his mind that he thinks he is seeing, clairvoyantly, a vision of his past life, when in fact, it is just a trick of the mind. What he saw and felt was a vision or impression brought to him by his Indian Guide, who remembers so clearly how he lived when he was on earth.

This example comes from the writer's own experience. I can recall several times in my life when I have suddenly felt much taller, and sensed in a peculiar way the solitary stillness of a dark forest. The mental impression was so clear that it would be easy for me to imagine that in one of my past lives on earth I was a tall, powerful Indian Chief. However, after one of these experiences, my guide, 'Red Chief, spoke to me through Walsh and said that what I had experienced was HIS presence and HIS memory.

The philosophy of reincarnation can be harmful to some as it could lead to negative fatalism. This occurs when a person excuses the condition he is in—a condition, perhaps, of self-inflicted misery and failure—as a punishment for some past life on earth. Such a person may not make sufficient effort to rise out of this condition.

The only truth about the reality of reincarnation resides in the simple fact that when the spirit of man has progressed to the Eleventh Plane and has thus reached the Light of God, his purified spirit becomes part of that Light of God. Thus when a spark of this pure Light of God returns to enter into the body of a newly born infant, that man's purified spirit will be fractionally returned to earth, but only 'fractionally'. In this sense PART of man does eventually reincarnate.

If a vessel of water is taken from a creek, purified, and then poured into a lake of purified water, it becomes an integral part of that lake. So, if another empty vessel is dipped into this lake of pure water, that fraction of water taken will, in its purest sense, be that contained in the original vessel.

Man and woman through union reproduce their species, but that which is reproduced is not that man or woman—it is another individual with its own personality. The flesh and blood reproduced is made up of past generations of their ancestors, likewise the various traits of character.

So, in the spirit, when the purified soul of man at last goes back INTO the Light of God from where it originally came, there is reproduced from this Light of God a spark of pure Light to return to the earth. But it is a NEW spark, a NEW soul. It is not the original soul of that man or woman who has already lived on this earth.

What is meant by the 'Eleven Planes of Light' in the Spirit World?

Actually it should be called the eleven 'states' of spiritual understanding.

When souls pass into the spirit world they graduate to the spiritual plane according to the state of spiritual understanding which they had developed on earth. By 'understanding', is meant the 'understanding' of a loving heart.

Souls go neither to Hell nor straight to Heaven. There is no Hell, but there is a state of darkness where those who have led evil, selfish lives, go. This darkness in which they are enveloped when they first pass over, is of their own making. They have turned a deaf ear to the higher thoughts of their true self, their soul. Instead, they have let their minds dwell on evil things and indulged in selfish thoughts and actions. They have let evilness rule their lives, and evilness is always born in darkness.

The Soul of Man is the spark of God's Light placed within him. By ignoring the still, small voice of their soul, they have turned their backs on the Light within, and so, lost their way in the darkened pathways of lust, greed, hate, selfishness and all that is unworthy of man's true destiny.

The first plane is one of darkness where these unprogressed spirits go. Eventually they are persuaded to progress by their guardian angels. While these unhappy ones dwelt on earth, their guardian angels found it difficult to influence their darkened minds for good. They can now help them more directly to rise, or come out of the darkness and rise to higher spheres. They are often influenced by the sincere, loving prayers of earthly mortals such as those sitting in spiritual circles, who understand the plight of these unfortunate ones. This helps them to repent, and lift themselves out of their gloomy surroundings.

Spirits who have led varying degrees of usefulness or goodness when on earth go to the spiritual plane corresponding to that degree. They do not go to Heaven immediately they pass over. Heaven is not one perfect state of beatitude suddenly acquired when a good soul rises from the dead. Heaven can only be likened, in an earthly way, to a beautiful high mountain which a soul climbs until it reaches its peak, which is called the Eleventh Plane.

As it climbs, the soul rests at various stations, called planes. Actually they are spiritual states of understanding. To whatever plane or station they go, they find, after a while, that they are met by 'Angels' or 'Angelic Spirits' from higher planes, who urge them to climb still higher—to climb spiritually, of course; there is no physical climbing in the spiritual realms.

These descriptions of progression upwards, from plane to plane, to a beatific state can be likened to the educational progression of dwellers on earth, from the time they are born until they reach manhood or womanhood. They are first sent to kindergarten, then to primary schools, from there they go, either to high school or technical schools according to their desires or abilities, and, if they wish to, finally strive to enter a university. After years of hard study at a university, they are awarded a Degree. This wordly Degree is tantamount, in the spirit world, to being finally lifted up to the Eleventh Plane, where they experience the unutterable ecstasy and joy of dwelling forever with God.

The difference between this 'earthly' progression and 'spiritual' progression, is that EVERYONE in the spiritual realms, from the lowest of the low, has the opportunity of endeavouring to rise, stage by stage, until they have learned this 'spiritual' Degree—which is the Eleventh Plane of Light.

Is God an individual Spirit or Person?

No—God is ALL spirit, ALL power, ALL might, ALL light, ALL love, ALL life. Everything that is GOOD is GOD.

All that matters in God's sight, really, is a LOVING HEART, a Love symbolised in Christ's heart. A Loving Heart always tries to avoid hurting others, and to think of others before themselves.

The truth Relating to Birth, Life and Death

When God wills that a child is to be born through the seed of man and woman, the Light shines down upon the woman, and from out of that Light come twelve spirits of pure Light. These hover over the woman, and when the time is ready, one remains to be born and live on this earth. Only the flesh and blood are born of the parents. The Life, which is the Spirit, comes from God. That spark of Light or Spirit is the Soul. Even in the case of test tube babies or artificial insemination, the Spirit of Pure Light makes its entry 'when the time is ready'—that is, when the Seed, from or in the test tube, enters the Ovum and a new life begins.

For the first three years, the tender years of child life, it is guided by the remaining eleven spirits. After the third year the child comes to the understanding of worldly conditions, and until it is fourteen is guided by spirits or guardians of varying degree, ordained by God. But, at fourteen, a special guide is sent by God to be THE GUIDE OF HIS OR HER LIFE, called by Catholics, and rightly so, a Guardian Angel. In addition a person usually has many guides or spirit helpers to advise and guide them in various phases of their lives.

The chief guide, however, or Guardian Angel, who came to them in their fourteenth year, remains with them all through their lives. Often guides or helpers may be relatives or friends or a spirit guide who is interested in what that earthly person is doing or studying.

God gives to us free will, but there are certain milestones through which we must pass. This is planned by God before we are born. We cannot avoid these milestones planned in the original DIVINE BLUEPRINT of our lives, but, between them we are at liberty to do what our free will prompts us to do. We can always follow the dictates of our own will, or, likewise we have the freedom to choose to obey God's Will.

As we go through life, we are judged in everything that we do, say and think. But God is just. We are not judged by the day. WE ARE JUDGED BY OUR WHOLE LIFE. God sees and understands the hidden motives deep down within the soul of each one of us. There are conditions or handicaps often hidden from other men, which can mar one's life, but God sees these things and judges accordingly. His judgement is not like ours. We judge from what we can gather or see from the outside, but God looks into the heart and judges from what He can see within us. He, alone, can read and understand every hidden thought.

From the moment we are born, everything that we do, say and think is written in the 'Book of Life'. This book is held in the hands of God, but the handwriting is our OWN. When we go back to the Kingdom of God, we will be taken to a spiritual mansion, or home, which we have built by our thoughts and actions.

Good thoughts and deeds are represented, symbolically, by beautiful flowers of Light in one's mansion. Selfish or evil thoughts and acts will build darkness in the spiritual walls of this home. When the soul goes to its spiritual home and finds some of the walls marred with sin, it craves to wipe this ugliness out. This can be done by good deeds performed in the spirit world.

In due time, a soul will cleanse the walls of its mansion until they are perfect and it dwells in a home of pure Light.

At the moment called death—but which is actually re-birth—everything for a moment, is dark. In this moment in time comes the realisation that a change has taken place in the soul's existence. Then, out of the darkness the soul sees Light coming towards it. In that Light it sees loved ones, passed on before, eager to meet and guide it to its spiritual home or mansion as already mentioned.

According to the life lived on earth, so the soul progresses in the spiritual planes. There are Eleven Planes which it must pass through, before it reaches the Light of God. As it rises there are always those above, eager and ready to help it reach that Light.

As it passes through each plane, it casts off more and more of the conditions that were gathered on earth. Finally all earthly conditions are shed, and the soul reaches the Light of God, from whence it came.

The importance of Mental Prayer—personal and corporate

The practice of mental prayer is of the greatest importance to the individual. Through it, the soul is strengthened and developed to such an extent that it is able, eventually, to effectively control, to a great degree the selfish desires and actions of the lower self.

If mental prayer becomes a habit it has a great impact on the life we live. All habits acquired, whether good or bad, begin on the conscious level. If the habit persists it gradually sinks into the subconscious. In other words the subconscious 'takes over' this conscious habit and continues to practise it, often without the conscious mind being aware of it.

As an example: the first time a person swears, he does so deliberately, but if he continues to do so, it becomes a habit, and in course of time all his conversation is sprinkled with oaths without the conscious mind realising this fact. This applies also to the consciously acquired habit of smoking, drinking and so on.

It stands to reason, therefore, that the habit of mental prayer will, likewise, sink into the subconscious, and one's whole life becomes a living prayer without one realising it. The Apostle Paul urged his followers to pray without ceasing, which seems impossible, but it IS possible, if mental prayer becomes a habit, simply because the subconscious carries on with the praying habit, while the conscious mind is occupied with its everyday, mundane tasks.

It affects, not only our everyday thoughts unknowingly, but also our everyday behaviour, both at home and in our work-a-day life. Our success in life, both spiritually and materially, is dependent, more than we realise, on the development of our soul (which modern-day man calls the 'subconscious'). This development, through mental prayer, is a vital force, a force that enables us to overcome all sorts of seemingly impossible obstacles. It was this constant practice of mental prayer that inspired great souls of the past, in every walk of life to do many extraordinary things; to endure all sorts of imaginable hardships or suffering and to make what seemed impossible possible.

To know and to do God's will is the secret of true happiness, because only God knows what is best for you in every eventuality. Mental prayer is the doorway that leads to a growing awareness, day by day, of God's will in life.

Often you may know, inwardly, what is right and just, for you to do, but may lack the courage or strength of will to do it. Mental prayer gives you that strength, in spite of the vehement urging of your lower self, to do what is contrary, and in the end, disastrous.

It also helps you to understand yourself. The hardest person in the world to understand is yourself. Until you understand yourself, you cannot understand God, for God is within you. Prayer helps you to acquire this understanding.

The habit of daily mental prayer not only helps with your own progression, but you find yourself, eventually, starting to pray for others. The more you progress inwardly through prayer, the more you can effectively pray for others.

Prayer opens the door of your soul and enables the Love and Light from God to flow into your being to strengthen and inspire you in everything you do, privately and socially. When you start praying for others, that same Love and Light of God shines from you and touches all whom you name in your prayers.

At the same time as you pray for those in need, naming them in your heart, you are also, without knowing it, praying also for hundreds whom you do not know by name. The power of God, flowing from you, not only helps those whom you name, but it flows on and touches the souls of many more who may be in distress, so that they, too, are healed or blessed by God through your prayers. Eventually your prayer returns to you, blessing you a hundredfold for what you have done for others—through your faith in God.

Corporate mental prayer is, also, of very great importance. It has been neglected far too much, of late, by the Orthodox Christian Church, with the result that the Church is not as effective as it should be in the hidden life of the community. One day the practice of weekly prayer meetings will again become a very important feature in the life of the Church. They are the life blood of all churches.

This is, in essence only, what we were taught on mental prayer. The original messages were expressed in beautiful language, but hard to record, so the author has summarised it in modern terms.

No meeting was complete unless the members of Walsh's circles prayed silently for the sick, the lost and all in distress, giving specific names as well. Usually ten to fifteen minutes were set aside for this purpose. Often as we prayed, mentally, at the instigation of one of the guides, the Light would begin to shine through the hands of the instrument, or through various parts of his body, as a sign that the collective prayer was going out of the room.

Weak or unprogressed spirits, spirits who were lost or in great darkness, were continually brought to our meetings by the guides to be encouraged and helped on the road to progression and peace. Whenever an unhappy spirit, or lost soul, controlled the instrument, his or her name was ascertained and each member of the circle would promise to pray for them also in the silence of their own homes.

In this way, thousands of lost souls throughout those years were, t

25

THE PURPOSE OF IT ALL

Men are but children of a larger growth

Dryden

It is necessary at this stage to answer a question often put to me by orthodox Christians, and others who have never witnessed psychic phenomena. It is a good question and deserves a clearly defined answer. In essence, it is: 'Granted that all you say about these meetings or séances is true, what did they, in fact, achieve or accomplish? From what we hear, conversations between sitters and those from the spirit world were often trivial, or of little importance; various objects were carried around the room, instruments were played, the trumpet or megaphone flew here, there and everywhere, and there was quite a lot of talking, laughing, and exchange of questions and answers, but what was it all about? Furthermore what did it prove to those who listened and has it really helped them?'

The simple answer is: 'It helped many to know God better. It helped others to find or understand Him. Especially those who may never have known or understood Him. It also helped some to find the God they had rejected.'

Then it might be asked: Do you mean to tell me, when a spirit plays a banjo, or a toy piano, or speaks through a trumpet or a medium that THIS helps these enquirers to find God?

The answer is: exactly! Let me explain. Many of those who come to séances are 'spiritual infants'! They may be fine, upright, strong characters, successful in life, trustworthy, honest and so one, but have no belief in God, or understanding of Him. Spiritually they are infants! A lot of the physical phenomena may appear trivial or seemingly over simple but should be seen in comparison to that of a little child when it first commences its education. In the initial stages of education a child plays with coloured blocks, paints and is given simple little exercises or trained in rhythmic movements, such as waving their hands to and fro and singing 'my hands are waving'. This is all very trivial to mature minds, but there is a definite purpose and planning behind it. A study of books on child psychology will explain this.

When a person learns elocution, public speaking, or singing, he engages in certain breathing exercises, twists and wags his jaws vigorously up and down, or says aloud: 'Pee Bee—Tee Dee—Tay Day—Pay Bay' to improve his articulation, or sings simple scales. You may find him standing in front of a mirror where he draws his shoulders back, throws out his chest and brings his right hand with a sweeping gesture until it is directly above his head, or you may see him walking up and down, balancing a heavy book on the top of his head! Silly, isn't it? But this is essential training for correct deportment.

What happens when you learn to swim, even if an adult? The instructor first makes you wiggle your feet up and down in a scissors motion—but why go on? The first stages in any training or study appear to be trivial, or infantile, but there are definite reasons for these apparent trivialities. They prepare the trainee for more serious things.

Returning to the question we can see that, as in training for earthly occupations, so it must be in spiritual matters. The same technique, in essence, was used by the High Guides of Stan Walsh. They worked always to a set plan or pattern. There was one purpose—the progress of souls, •either in the spirit world, or still on the earth plane. The idea was simple: All strangers allowed into séances by the guides were given absolute proof, in some form or other, of life after death. Eternity was shown as an actual reality—and the proof always was of a personal nature.

After they had recovered from their surprise on their first night, visitors were invited again, and further proof, messages or consolation from those in the spirit world would be always given to them.

At the same time, the guides would be giving their lectures and gradually teaching newcomers the Truth Of God. This would embrace not only the truth about life after death, but the fact that God is a God of Love. They would learn that we have to answer to God through our own true selves for the life we live on earth; that all souls, no matter how low they have fallen, are eventually saved; that Jesus Christ is the true and only Son of God, and the Saviour of the whole world; that in Christ we all live.

All strangers were given the same spiritual tuition to supply knowledge and understanding that they often lacked, commencing with the kindergarten experience of spirit voices, moving objects, acrobatic trumpet, and so on. From these simple discoveries, little manifestations of basic truths, and symbols they were gradually drawn to higher and higher knowledge, until their faith was restored—or awakened. I lost count of those, including myself, who were turned towards God over those years.

All religious leaders agree that the salvation of the world rests upon the salvation of the individual. The work of the churches is to concentrate on the individual and to give him the spiritual nourishment that he needs— but not all individuals can be given spiritual nourishment out of the same dish. As a world famous entertainer once said, 'One man's cornbeef is another man's ulcers'.

Atheists, agnostics, sophisticates, and all those who are completely indifferent to any form of spirituality are spiritually infantile.

Religious leaders will tell you that a man or woman who has reached the age of twenty-five or thirty years without any religious training, finds it almost impossible to develop a belief in God.

This means that these 'spiritual children', as I have chosen to call them, can only be given the chance of progression on this earth plane by a miracle, or through unorthodox channels.

Many hundreds of people over the years, between 1919 to 1939, experienced that miracle when they were brought along to Walsh's meetings. They were, in most cases, 'spiritual infants'! They commenced their spiritual training in the first grade—through spirit voices and all kinds of minor psychic phenomena as already mentioned.

I remember one young man who came along to these séances in 1932.

He was Bruce Connan and his personal testimony can be found at the end of this book. He was a dentist, clever, and bright, but inclined to be a little wild and a confirmed atheist.

He was given remarkable evidential messages from his mother in spirit —one whom he had dearly loved. He was so impressed by all this that he brought along his brother, then, later, a friend. They were enthralled by the spirit voices, the whirling trumpet and other objects. They exchanged breezy conversation with the spirit children and one or two humorous spirit personalities such as Gus Bluett, who, on earth, had been a popular Australian comedian, and, the irrepressible Guide, Hetty.

Gradually the wonderful lectures of the guides began to claim their attention more and more. In time their characters were definitely steadied and these three set them on the right path. Today, they are fine middle-aged citizens each with a simple faith in God which nothing can shake.

One of them is now a Justice of the Peace, a Rotarian and a very fine example giving Christian man.

Christ told Peter that he would make him a fisher of men. His successors are found today not only in the orthodox churches, but also in many séance rooms where those few sincere and truthful mediums dedicate their lives to demonstrating, usually in the privacy of their own homes, that there is a God—a God of Love, that there is no death.

A genuine spiritual medium is indeed also a fisher of men! But the bait that he or she uses is quite different from that used by orthodox churches.

It is an unorthodox bait—a bait which has proved especially irresistible to men and women who would never, under any circumstances, enter an orthodox church—at least, not before they 'met God' in an unorthodox way.

A famous theologian once said that 'religion is not taught, it is caught'.

In the epilogue of this book are suggestions on how to continue to use this unorthodox bait to catch those who have lost their way.

26

HIS TASK WELL DONE

Nunc Dimittis

LUKE 2:29-32

Early in 1939 Walsh was ill. He spent a week at a country guesthouse at Kallista with his family. Jones and I went up there for the weekend.

He had suffered much pain, and it was thought a few days in the country might help. One night we were walking along the passage when he walked out of his room and asked us to come in. As we did he told us to look at his bed. He turned out the light and as we looked, we saw a large white luminous cross covering his bed.

He said he had been lying down for a few hours, trying to get ease from the pain, and he had felt the guides magnetizing his body. Gradually he felt relief coming from their ministrations. It was then that he thought his bed was lit up with a strange glow.

'I wonder why it came?, said Jones. I echoed his words.

Walsh shook his head. 'I don't know,' he replied; he appeared very depressed.

A few months later we understood.

In spite of the adulation and wonder he aroused in a never ending stream of visitors to his meetings, Stan Walsh became increasingly, a lonely man. His spirit was out of his body so much that he was as one poised between two worlds, in neither one nor the other. Inwardly he became more and more like the eagle, solitary and alone. Like Moses on Mount Sinai, he was sometimes high above the crowd beneath, and yet below the Glory of God.

During the last ten years of his life, Walsh, like the other members of the Inner Circle, had become a man of prayer. This had developed in response to the teachings of the High Guides. They constantly stressed the importance of mental prayer for the continual advancement of the powers of the Inner Circle, and for our individual progression. They taught us to practise mental prayer, not only at our meetings, but also in the privacy of our own homes.

Mental prayer is entirely different from vocal prayer. It was through the teachings of these great spiritual guides on this subject that I began to study books on it. There are quite a number written. One of the best is, *The Ways of Mental Prayer*, 1930, M. H. Gill, Dublin, by Dom Lehodey, a French abbot. There are others, by both Catholic and Protestant authors.

Everyone who seeks to develop psychic gifts should regard the practice of mental prayer as a 'must'.

Walsh was always praying for the highest helpers to come down to the meetings, and he constantly prayed personally for each of his followers.

Prayer so occupied him that, accomplishing the Will of God became, increasingly, his only aim in life.

As time went on the pressure of these great spiritual forces bearing down upon him, and through him, brought fatigue to body and mind. His health began to deteriorate.

His family did not understand his spiritual work. They urged him to give it all up, but he was deaf to their pleas. The 'work' came first. He realised, as his followers did, that the Light shining through his body at every meeting, in so many different ways, was shining OUT from the meetings, into the world, and bringing peace and strength into the lives of many.

At times, there are thoughts, deep down within us all, that we find impossible to explain or reveal to anyone but God. There are problems to be solved, or hard decisions to be made which can only be discussed with God. This, of course, only applies to those who have faith in God, irrespective of their particular religion, cult or creed. Those who have no faith, or cannot believe there is a God, often have to take these deep thoughts to a psychologist who can sometimes help. For the believer, however, God can give the right answer. Only God understands us completely. Often this answer is brought down to us, in His name, by our guardian angel or spiritual guide.

Such was the case with Stan Walsh. Although he did not confide to a soul what passed between him and his Maker, I know, from one or two confidential remarks made by him, that he was determined that God was to be first and last in everything he did.

Like us all, Walsh was given free will. HE COULD, AT ANY TIME, HAVE WITHDRAWN FROM HIS MISSION AND STOPPED THE LIGHT SHINING THROUGH HIM. He could have gone back to a normal life again, and, undoubtedly, lived for many years longer.

But like so many of the great saints of history, Stan's great love was for God. This increased over the years and drove him to the point where he was ready to sacrifice his life so that others might benefit from the Power of God available through him.

When Christ was brought before the Sanhedrin on trial for His life, and there was much argument, Caiaphas the High Priest, stood up and said:

'Ye know nothing at all, nor consider that it is expedient for us, that one man should die for the people...' John: 11.50

Walsh, like many prophets of the past, was caught up by the love of God, a love that gave ALL, without any exception.

The story of Walsh's love of God, is the same old story, and the same act of complete selflessness, which has been enacted in the hearts of many great souls throughout the ages.

During the last year, or so, loneliness and sacrifice were his constant companions, and pain and weariness sat on his pillow at night.

It was a rare thing to guides to prophesy anything, by referring to specific dates. As already said, time over there does not exist, and is, consequently, hard to calculate in relation to earth time, but at a Sunday meeting in September 1939, Malocca came through and asked us all to watch 28th October, and seven days after that. The meeting was held in Jones's big dining room and there were over thirty present. We all wondered what Malocca meant.

When we told Walsh, he remained silent and seemingly depressed. On 28th October Walsh was taken to the hospital for a surgical operation. That same day I married a second time, and Stan had promised to be best man at our wedding.

My wife, Anne, and I called on him before we left on our honeymoon. Anne brought an armful of flowers from the wedding reception. As he lay in bed and we prepared to go, he took both our hands in his and said: I'll come back and bless you both always.' We really thought he meant he would come and visit us, at our home, when he was better.

Several days after the operation, Stan's condition became worse. Mrs Lehman was among the many friends who visited him during those days It was in her home that he first began his meetings. She told me later, that as she was about to leave him she said: 'I'll come and see you again soon, Stan.'

'No, don't come,' he said, 'I won't be here.'

'Oh, are you going home soon?' she asked.

He hesitated with a slightly puzzled look on his face, then smiled and said: 'Yes, that's right. I'm going home.'

He went 'Home' on 4th November, 1939, exactly seven days after 28th October, as Malocca had said.

The Light that had shone through this human lamp throughout the years, and brought so much joy and happiness to many, eventually brought darkness, for just a moment, to the faithful instrument.

Of his own free will, he let that Light enter his body and stay there until its unearthly brightness destroyed the body, but not the soul. That lives on forever.

After the night, came the dawn, bringing back the Light to his soul, and lifting it up into everlasting Eternity, where that Light never fades nor grows dim.

27

A CROSS OF LIGHT

He is not here—He is risen

MARK 16-6

Walsh's death was a great shock to us all, especially to Bert Jones. They had been inseparable friends for twenty years. The night before the burial service Bert was deeply distressed. He told me that as he was sitting dejectedly on his bed, he was greatly consoled by a message he received, clairaudiently, from Malocca. Walsh's guide told him that his friend had been lifted up to a very high plane of Light and rewarded by God with a joy that was unspeakable.

At the burial service at Brighton Cemetery a huge crowd gathered, followers past and present. Many came from distant places and country towns. The minister who conducted the burial service was the Reverend Hamilton, of the Dorcas Street Church of England in South Melbourne—the church where Stan had seen a vision of angels as a choirboy long ago. Before the service at Walsh's home the Reverend Hamilton, told Mrs Walsh, that 'he considered it a great privilege to be conducting the service'. He had heard from several quarters over the years of the wonderful work for God that her son had accomplished throughout his life. They were words that brought great comfort to his mother.

There was one strange occurrence at his home. His body was lying in the open coffin in his bedroom as was the custom in those days. The night before his burial his sister, Norma, happened to pass the room and noticed a faint glow coming from the darkness. She walked in and saw, to her astonishment, a cross of Light covering his body. She went out and told her mother and elder sister, Olive. When they came into the darkened room the cross had disappeared. Naturally they said she must have imagined it. But Norma, a very practical type of person, strenuously asserted that she did see it. She is still alive and asserts this to this day.

Like her parents she had never witnessed his spiritual work, and was not too sure why this cross had been shown to her. However when I explained to her later about the Lighted Cross which often appeared at out meetings, she understood.

A few weeks after his funeral some of his followers, including my wife and myself, held weekly meetings at Bert's home in Newmarket. They were more in the nature of prayer meetings, in which we endeavoured to practise what the guides had taught us, that is, the importance of Mental Prayer.

We put the trumpet in the circle for a few sessions, hoping it would move, but it didn't. We realised that the direct voice gift was Stan's and died with his physical body.

Inspiration messages came to some of the sitters. Bert had always had the gift of clairaudience. The result was that, now and then, messages were received through Bert or one or two of the others. Messages came from Stan that he was very happy and would continue to come down from time to time to help us in our daily life. Each week we would give names of people we heard were ill, or needed help, and pray for them. But after a few months through departure of some to distant places, the meetings broke up.

Bert continued to come to our place once a week for dinner and we would spend the evening talking of our experiences over the years at Stan's meetings. Sometimes we would concentrate for half an hour in prayer; Bert, myself and my wife. Often Bert had a message for us, either from Stan or one of the guides. This bond of friendship continued for some years.

Then, one evening early in 1950 I received a phone call which shocked my beyond measure. Bert's nephew rang to say that his uncle had been knocked down by a car in Russell Street, Melbourne. He had been taken to the Melbourne Hospital, he said, and died several hours later.

A week or so later I was writing quietly in my study, when I suddenly heard, inwardly, Bert's voice say: 'I have been waiting a long time for this, now I am happy.' Of the original five members of the Inner Circle, one member only is left, myself.

Mrs Martin, shortly after Walsh's death, shifted from Albert Park to the country. She was a wonderful person. I was always welcome in her home at Albert Park, and we were very dear friends. She died some years later. Mabel Grenville, the fourth member, died in the Alfred Hospital in 1953. I used to visit her at her home in Balaclava for some years prior to her illness. We would hold one hour prayer meetings. Sometimes I received inward messages during our mental silences, mostly of a personal nature, either from Stan or one of the guides. Very rare, very brief, but to the point.

When she was taken ill and sent to the hospital I called on her a day or so later. She said to me: 'Les, the Sister says that I will be undergoing a major operation to-morrow, but I know my time has come. I saw the spirit of a man and two women near my bed last night. I couldn't see them very clearly, but I think it was my mother and father, and my sister, Edie, coming for me. I'm not worried, it's God's will.' Then she smiled at me and like the typical casual Australian that she was, said: 'I'll remember you to Stan and Bert and the others, when I go over.' I bent down and kissed her on the forehead, and said, 'Cheerio, Mabel', and she replied, with a smile, 'au revoir'.

Next day she was operated on, but it was obvious that it was too much for her. When I called to see her after the operation she did not know me, and was sinking. The next day she went 'Home', too.

Over the years I have sometimes received messages from 'Beyond'. In 1942, three years after Stan's death I joined the Presbyterian Lay Preachers Association, and preached in Presbyterian and Methodist Churches for many years, also now and then in Spiritualist churches. During that time, the messages I received, clairaudiently, were very encouraging. On one occasion Mrs Martin spoke to me. She said: 'Keep up the good work, Les'. On another occasion I heard inwardly the voice of Mabel say: 'I'll help you, Les.' Sometimes I heard Stan's voice, with one or two messages of a very personal nature. On one occasion he urged me to take on daily mental prayer, which I eventually did.

Although those wonderful experiences of Walsh's mediumship have long since gone, his work is by no means finished. Those who knew him and are alive today, still feel the magnetic power of God's love and wisdom coming to us through this 'Man of God.'

28

AN INSPIRATION TO CARRY FORWARD

> I believe there are spiritual guides, mystic helpers, guardian angels
>
> THE REV. SIR IRVING BENSON, D.D.

The above declaration was made by the Rev. Sir Irving Benson several years ago in an article he wrote for the Melbourne Herald. The article was headed: "Angels Need Not Have Wings". Those who read this article must have been heartened by what he wrote, especially Christians who attend church regularly, and could do with more inspiring words like these.

It is thought, nowadays, that the church is losing its grip; that it is becoming a little bit 'old hat'; that it is getting out of touch with the very real problems of modem times and the pitfalls and confusions of our so called 'permissive' society.

One of the problems of communication in modern management is the tendency of leaders to rely too much on typed memos to their subordinates. That authority on Industrial Psychology, Eric Moorman, suggests that in the conduct of business, effective personal relations are better maintained by speaking 'man to man', rather than by memo.

This is true, not only in the world of business, but also in the spiritual sphere. Countless 'memos' have been written about man's direct experiences with God, His Son, Jesus Christ and His Angels. Every now and then, however, God finds it necessary to send His Angels to again speak through the lips of man to assure His people that most of the 'memos' written about Him are true.

Walsh was one of these chosen men through whom the Angels of God spoke. Today this personal touch is again needed. The sacred message must not come in a flamboyant, mercenary way, but expressed by chosen people. That is, through sincere, gifted mediums who are prepared to offer their services, gratis, to the Church. This is not an impossible idea. What is there to stop a truly gifted medium offering his or her services to the Church in the same manner as other dedicated people such as Social Workers, Charity Organisers, Youth Leaders, and Teachers? It would be vital of course that such an offer be made with no thought of mercenary gain whatsoever.

Unfortunately, the study of spirit evidence has had little encouragement from the established churches. Many good church-going people, especially Christians, feel a sense of guilt in taking any sort of interest in spiritual subjects other than those laid down in their own liturgies, or their own prayer books, or under the guidance of their own ministers or priests.

And yet as early as during the life of Pope Pius X, Catholics were given a certain degree of freedom in exploring scientific spirit evidence. Dr Godfrey Raupert of London was delegated by Pope Pius X to lecture in America on the subject, and to the Catholic audiences there he said, in substance: 'It is no longer possible to put the subject of psychic phenomena aside. Scientific men all over the world have now recognised spiritism as a definite and real power and to shelve it would be a dangerous policy. The Pope has asked me to tell Catholics the attitude they should take on it, that is, that the Church admits the reality of these phenomena and their external intelligences; in fact it has always admitted this reality. The problem is to discover the nature of the intelligences. We are now on the borderline of new discoveries which may revolutionise the world. We must admit dangers in the study of a subject as new as spiritism, but to have only partial knowledge of the subject would be more dangerous. We must suspend judgement of the subject until it is better known.'

Among many of the pioneers in psychic research are clergymen of various denominations of the Christian religion, and some of the most serious and successful research into spiritual phenomena today is in the hands of devout and sincere Christians.

Places like the Christian College of Madras have produced some extraordinary results along with the findings of Professor C. T. K. Chari on extra-sensory perception, clairvoyance, and the fact that there is in operation a 'strange capacity in some form more powerful than we have as yet perceived.'

What is there in this freer thinking, more open minded age to stop the linking up of genuine mediums, who hold properly conducted services in the privacy of their own homes, to the services of the Church? This could especially benefit church members who suffer bereavement and sorely need God's comfort in this way. Such services could easily be conducted under strict control of a wise and understanding minister.

Churches have their various Clubs, Guilds, Charitable Associations, Pentecostal Movements, Open Forums, etc. Why not a 'Psychic Fellowship'? As the Priest or Minister reads out the announcements, setting out dates and times of meetings of the above, why not include the following: 'On Thursday evening at 7.30 p.m. there will be the usual meeting of the Psychic Fellowship under the mediumship of Mrs X.'

In fact, the Church IS beginning to take more interest in genuine psychic truths. Norman Peale D.D., in his book, *The Power of Positive Thinking*, Heinemann, 1953, England, writes: 'Scientists working today in the field of parapsychology, and extra sensory perception (ESP) and experimenting in pre-cognition (Prophesying), telepathy and clairvoyance ... are expressing themselves as believing that the Soul survives Death.'

He then goes on to give specific instances where professed Christians of the Orthodox Church have experienced in their own homes, definite evidence of human survival.

Today in England, there is a tendency, rapidly growing, for Church of England ministers to hold services in private homes, away from the Church. The Catholic Church is also doing this in many places. Why not private home séances under the auspices of the Church, conducted by mediums of high calibre and Christian outlook; mediums whose only motive is altruistic?

Among the great Truths enunciated in the Apostles' Creed is the belief in the Communion of Saints. Would it not be possible to demonstrate this truth in private homes as related above?

If this is so, how should a genuine home circle be conducted? This is discussed in the last chapter of this book.

29

A PRACTICAL PLAN

Try and Trust will move mountains

OLD PROVERB

Let me refer again to the brilliant, industrial psychologist, Eric Moorman, who suggests that there are limits to the success of any organisation unless it satisfies human needs. The Orthodox church has, always aimed to satisfy human needs. It has achieved this, up to a point, but not quite all the way. To convince mankind that human survival after death is an absolute fact, is a real human need. As mentioned before in this book, the Churches are now beginning to recognise that on the spot evidence of life hereafter is a real need.

Their problem is: How can this 'need' be satisfied? The answer is that this can be accomplished only by genuine, dedicated mediums who are prepared to give their services to these churches in an honorary capacity.

Nowadays there are not enough genuine mediums to go round. Leaving out of consideration those whose sole desire, in consulting mediums, is to have their fortunes told repeatedly, there are many earnest people, Christian and otherwise, who mourn those they have lost and are eager and ready to be convinced of their survival, if genuine, evidential results are forthcoming. Only gifted mediums of a high calibre can do this. With insufficient mediums, how can this urgent need be fulfilled? The answer is in the formation and development of private home circles.

Mediumship is a very sensitive plant. It has to be brought to fruition as a rare exotic flower. It needs to grow in the protected hothouse of a private home, and in the congenial flowerpot of a quiet room. Here, surrounded with the soil of sympathy, love and patience, and fertilised with the sincere prayers and faith of those who attend these meetings, the sensitive mediumistic plant can be perfected.

I am firmly convinced beyond all doubt, after a lifetime study of psychic phenomena in all its various forms, that it is not an art, an accomplishment, or a science. It is a religion, with God as its foundation stone. It is upon this stone that those who want to become mediums must build.

This being so, the question arises: Is it God's Will that he or she should develop as a medium? The word 'religion', I know, contains emotional overtones which are associated with hypocrisy, dogmatism, bigotry, superstition and intolerance, but true Christians of every denomination are convinced that the true definition of 'religion' is actually a belief in spiritual truths. And the first essential of human survival is to realise that it is a Divine Truth, that God's love is so great that He would never commit anyone to senseless oblivion.

Mediumship is a gift often latent within the soul, or subconscious mind. That is why it is most important that the psychic aspirant first finds out whether to develop in this direction is a Divine purpose.

The gift of mediumship carries with it great responsibilities. It can bring great joy to those who use it for the benefit of mankind, but it also involves danger and unhappiness to those who take it on lightly, or try to develop it for other than truly altruistic reasons.

If we accept the fact that God is spirit and that our soul is a Divine spark, what does that imply? It means that this vital spark is your real self. As you are part of the Divine spirit it is obvious that God can speak to you direct, if He so desires, without any intermediary, such as a guide or spirit friend. There are rare moments in your life when some great thought or idea, or question of importance literally takes possession of you, something which may alter the whole course of your life. Often the sincerity and depth of your feelings in this matter may make it impossible for you to explain them to anyone, even to those closest to you. In your dilemma, your earnest thoughts, or quest for an answer, turn inwardly to something deep down, to the God within you.

Your deep inward quest means that you are actually speaking to God. If what you ask for is true and sincere, then God speaks to you—direct. Sincere, honest searching is soul questioning. And God always speaks to the soul, which is sincere, not to the conscious mind. Eventually, however, what God has said within slowly rises out of the unconscious into the conscious mind. Often, in a flash, you know what you should do. You are then convinced beyond doubt, though often you find it difficult to explain to others why you are convinced. You cannot always give reasons for your final decision because God has spoken to you.

You might say: 'but I have never actually heard God's voice speak to me. I have heard spirit voices, or I have had impressions given to me by loved ones or guides in the spirit world, but never God's voice.' When I say, 'God speaks to you'—and, incidentally, this applies to all references to God 'speaking' in the Bible—I mean that God places thoughts in your soul. He speaks through thought-transference. Do not forget that God is spirit, that His thoughts are pure and completely divorced from personality or voice idiosyncrasies of individual spirit entities.

Pure thought, like pure music, does not arouse emotions, or sensual images, or a particular style. So it is hard to pin these deep thoughts on to a special spirit entity or guide. As God speaks to that part of God within you, you cannot distinguish your own deep thoughts from God's thoughts.

In other words, through earnest heart searching and probing within, you have found God. In such cases, your interchange of thoughts with God make it difficult for you to recognise God's thoughts from your own. In those solemn, earnest moments you and God are one. But you must be sincere. The Bishop of Woolwich in his book: *Honest to God*, SCM Press, London, was right when he said: 'To find God we must be earnest and sincere'.

Why have I stressed all this so much? Because this is the attitude of mind that must eventually be reached by one who aspires to be a medium. As the old proverb says: You must 'Trust in God and Try', without ceasing, to comply always with His Will.

Once you are firmly convinced beyond all doubt that you are right in starting a home circle, the next step is to form one. Seek out close friends, or members of the family you think are suitable. Be sure, if they agree to help you, that their motives, too, are sincere, that they have a real desire to know the truth and to help you to the utmost. At the same time it may be advisable to seek out a reliable medium, and see if he or she confirms what you think. It may be that, not you altogether, but someone whom you have called to your circle will develop mediumship. If so, give that person all the love and encouragement of your heart to help that person to develop. It may be that your task is to organise and create a home circle, not so much to develop your own psychic powers, but to be a pillar of strength to the one chosen to be the doorway between the two worlds.

No home circle should be started unless the members chosen are imbued with an earnest desire to help with their prayers, and seek only the Truth. To start a circle 'just for fun or out of mere curiosity' or to see what they get, is to invite trouble. Each member of the group needs to have a level head, to be devout, and to have both feet well and truly planted on the ground.

With patience, you will eventually find the right sitters. You want at least four members, but not more than five. Harmony can be better maintained with a small group than with one too large. It is imperative that each member should be imbued with the importance of sympathetic thoughts at these meetings. An embryo medium is far more sensitive to thought vibrations than those of an ordinary person.

How Should the Home Circle First Begin to Operate?

What should its members do? Should they engage an experienced, reliable medium to help its development?

The necessity of engaging a reputable medium for the opening meeting is essential. She or he can tell you the names of the guides who come to help, the length of time you should sit and routine to be established. But it is most important that the medium engaged must be beyond all doubt, a genuine, devout, fully developed medium. It is not necessary for her to come each week. The presence of a medium in a private circle each week may tend to divert the sitters from their original purpose that is, to foster psychic development for the upliftment of their fellow man, whether on this earth or on the darkened planes of the spirit world.

If the medium was present each week at these sittings, there would be a tendency, inherent in us all, to satisfy curiosity about our private wishes for the future, and thus mar the atmosphere of selflessness which is so needful to bring the right developing conditions into the room.

If it is possible to secure the presence of the local minister or priest at these meetings, all the better. All home circles should start with prayer.

It should start with a brief, simple spoken prayer, then followed by silent, mental prayer as advocated in this book. A quiet hymn could be sung, and the circle, in its early stage, should be conducted more like an earnest prayer meeting. The sincerity behind these mental prayers and periods of silent concentration represents the cultivated and fertile ground, from which should spring up the seeds of psychic development lying latent, perhaps, in one or two of its members. Apart from this, however, prayer is of great help in developing character.

Your prayers not only influence others, but also yourself. They change you imperceptibly, both in thought and action. They bring you closer to your true self, the God within. Strength of character is vital in developing mediumship, and prayer, both private and corporate, helps you to truly know yourself, and thus protect you from self-deceit, which is such a subtle and unconscious pitfall in the development of this sensitive plant-mediumship.

Pitfalls In Mediumship.

Vanity and pride are stumbling blocks for all of us; the desire to be gazed at with awe and wonder by friends and to be noticed by others. Mediumship, especially where deep or semi-trance is concerned, and even inspirational sometimes, appeals to the tendency for exhibitionism lying dormant in us.

The dramatic silence of concentration in the séance room often brings to the surface these weaknesses in our nature. Those aspiring to mediumship should have no illusions about themselves, and frankly recognise the above weaknesses as a possibility. Vanity links with imagination, and latent histrionic abilities can lead to self-hypnosis. The actor within takes over, alters the tone of voice and facial expressions. Then from the subconscious mind flows a stream of knowledge that has been acquired from books. Self hypnosis of this nature can take hold of you to such an extent that you not only deceive listeners, but yourself.

However, these weaknesses in our nature, as already stated, can be definitely eradicated if we earnestly and sincerely pray without ceasing that God will help us to be true to ourselves in everything that we do, say and think.

We cannot all be mediums in a psychic sense, but often in an earthly sense. Although only one medium may develop out of a circle of four or five members, the others may develop in an entirely different way. The constant practice of selfless, earnest prayer often brings to light unforeseen gifts lying latent in the minds of the sitters. Gifts of writing, organizing ability, a tendency for sustained study in their every day lives of nursing, accountancy, medical development, development of dynamic energy needed to cope with a responsible position, and so on. In other words, it may be God's Will that the progress you have made spiritually as a faithful and steadfast helper in your home circle must go further. Such spiritual progress is made to overflow into your everyday life, and you find yourself gaining extraordinary skill, energy and inspiration in your everyday occupation or profession, whether man or woman.

The most important work accomplished by such a circle, however, is not always realised by those who attend them. I recall a lecture given by Vashti, an Egyptian Guide, through Stan Walsh, in which he said: 'Whenever a small band of earnest people meet to develop psychic gifts, they must not grow disheartened if no one develops right away, or nothing happens. Their prayers, if sincere and kindly, help many weak spirits brought to the room. Their loving thoughts go out like a searchlight and help others outside—in the world of man also—some perhaps whom they will never know or meet in this life.'

Eventually, however, these meetings may bear fruit, from a mediumistic point of view. Someone may develop a psychic gift, which is tested and proved beyond doubt as being genuine. In such cases steps should be taken to arouse the interest of local church authorities. If a minister or priest has attended these meetings, or knows and approves of them, it should be possible to incorporate these meetings into the programme of activities of the church already mentioned, and thus open the way for outsiders—that is, members of the church in question—to attend these meetings and receive comfort and consolation by communing with the saints. In this way the home circle, gathered under the wing of the Church, can continue to let the Light shine—unseen perhaps, but nevertheless real—just as Walsh did as the outstanding instrument used for this purpose in the 'twenties and 'thirties. The saints we communed with in those days, were not only those 'canonized', but also relatives and friends, who have led the 'good life' and passed on to the high spheres in the Kingdom of God.

In summing up, I am certain that one day, Spiritualism will be consumed by a cleansing fire, and that out of its ashes will arise, Phoenix-like, the fundamental Truth of God, THAT THERE IS NO DEATH.

Home circles or spiritual meetings can then take their rightful place within the portals of the Church Triumphant—the True Church which like the Soul of Man, can never die.

EYE WITNESSES

This is to certify that I knew Mr Stan Walsh for over 20 years. From 1918-1939—the year of his death.

I was a member of the inner circle which comprised Stan, Bert Jones, Alexander Martin, myself, and later (about 1926) the Author, Les Danby. During the séances I sat on one side of him, holding his right hand, and Mrs Martin sat on the other side holding his left hand.

I witnessed the gradual development of all his powers starting with Deep Trance, then materialisation of articles (or rapports) development of spiritual lights through his body and in the room, the materialisation of paints through his finger tips enabling him to paint many pictures sometimes in the course of a few minutes—even though he had no training in art whatsoever.

In my opinion, and the opinion of many who witnessed the amazing spiritual phenomena shown through his body, he was a Prophet sent by God to prepare the way or to bring the realisation to many that in this era in which we live Jesus Christ would return to the Earth as He promised. It may not be in my time, but it is possible that the young people of today before they die will witness His second coming. As a modern prophet he also brought down from God through Jesus the Christ the wonderful lights that we witnessed, not for our benefit alone, but for the benefit of thousands in the world whom we shall never meet or see on this earth.

Apart from this great gifts, Stan Walsh was a good, clean living, simple, God fearing gentleman and I considered it a great privilege to have known him and to be one of his close friends during those years.

Signed Mabel Grenville
143 Hawthorn Road,
Caulfield,
Melbourne.
Victoria.
Witness to signature E. I. Dunn,
3 Allfrey St., E. Brighton.

I take pleasure in recording that I knew Stan Walsh from about 1932 until 1939, similarly being well acquainted with his parents and sister, Norma, who comprised a very likeable family. I was fortunate in being numbered among his many personal friends and shared regular outings with him in addition to consistently attending his meetings three times weekly.

He was markedly unselfish and kindly in nature with little interest in monetary matters or material comfort and I can honestly say that his attitude in regard to his mediumistic gifts was completely altruistic.

Despite my personal regard for Stan, I was objective and critical in my attitude towards the phenomenal occurrences at his meetings; nevertheless I was convinced beyond any doubt that personalities, other than his own, were able to use his body in trance condition. They exhibited mental capacity and knowledge that was completely beyond his educational resources. I similarly witnessed repeated phenomena that could not be accomplished by physical means.

Signed G. B. Connan, J.P.
Lemtal Pty. Ltd.
702 Plenty Road,
Reservoir, N.19 Vic.
Witness A. J. Connan,
Clarisse Av. Montmorency.

I wish to certify that I knew Stan Walsh for many, many, years—actually from about 1928 until 1939 the year of his death.

All the things that Mr Danby has written about him in his book are true. I witnessed many wonderful things through his mediumship. He was more than a medium—He was a servant of God and brought great joy to my sister and myself and to hundreds who were brought to hear him. I hold apports of his which were materialised through his hands. I also witnessed the wonderful paintings which he gave and witnessed the paint colours coming through the fingertips of his hands.

I also had many, many conversations through the spirit trumpet with many of my own spirit relatives and many other spirits—and I was given remarkable proof, over and over again, of the genuineness of their messages and the reality of the life beyond.

Signed Ethel F. Scale
14 Stimson St.,
Guildford.
NSW.
Australia.
Witness to signature Myra Mitchell
12 Stimson Street
Guildford

I knew Stan Walsh for many years right up until the day of his death. He was not only a wonderful medium, but a very fine man, whose character and sincerity were beyond reproach.

He held meetings at my home in Thornburg for seven years. Many remarkable things happened at these meetings. Far more than related by Mr Danby in his book. Visitors flocked to his meetings from everywhere and from all walks of life. On some nights there would be over forty seated round the room. My husband and I had to remove most of the furniture from the lounge room, and get boards from outside and use them as benches right round the wall, to hold the sitters.

Mr Danby refers to the Light that shone from his body—one of my most vivid recollections in this regard was of a certain night when the light shone from his forehead and then, under control, the guide spread out his hands in front of him, with the open palms facing us, and the light shone straight from the centre of his palms.

Stan Walsh was not only a wonderful medium, he was more than that. I agree with Mr Danby that he was a prophet of modern times, whose main mission over and above all the manifestations shown through him, was to proclaim the Second Coming of Christ which is rapidly approaching.

Signed E. V. Matheson
55 Donaldson St., IVANHOE. Vic.
Witness Vera Burke

123 Were St.,
Middle Brighton

This is to certify that I knew Stan Walsh of Albert Park, Victoria, for many years. He held spiritual séances in my home for about 3 years. It was in my home that the first materialisation occurred. They first came in the form of black feathers. It was also during the time he held meetings in my home that the first painting came to him.

I have witnessed many wonderful manifestations of Mr Walsh's gifts—trance power, materialisations, painting and other spiritual gifts. I have no hesitation in declaring that his great powers, amazing as they were, came from God and were absolutely genuine. His personal character was beyond reproach in every way.

Signed E. C. Campbell
Main Road,
BELGRAVE.
Victoria.
Witness to Signature J. W. Spencer J.P.
 Address of Witness
Main Road, Tacoma

I was for many years a sitter in the séance room where Mr Walsh's mediumship was revealed.

The voices, the materialisations, the paintings and the wonderful lights that issued from his body as explained in Mr Danby's book were all witnessed by me.

I received many evidential messages, also, through the trumpet and also through Mr Walsh's trance powers.

Many of the things I, and others, saw would have to be seen to be believed.

He was undoubtedly one of the greatest mediums of this age.

Signed Ada E. Hunter
42 Bridge Road,
Moorabbin. Vic.
Witness Nellie C. Camock, Alice Littlewoods
Address 42 Spring Road, Moorabbin

This is to certify that I knew Stan Walsh for many years. He was a very good friend to me and gave me a lot of fatherly advice and help. I met him about the year 1932 when I was 17 years of age. I attended his séances from then onward until his death in 1939. I witnessed all the incidents described in Mr Danby's book.

I do not think there has ever been another spiritual medium quite like him during the last two decades. His gifts were quite unique beyond all doubt, and his character was beyond reproach.

I am prepared to certify personally to his remarkable powers at any time if so desired.

> Signed Mr R. L. Collins
> Address 34 Belmont Avenue,
> Upney. Vic.
> Witness to signature.
> C. Light
> Address 2I Barton Avenue,
> Femtree Gully.

Paperbacks also available from White Crow Books

Elsa Barker—*Letters from a Living Dead Man*
ISBN 978-1-907355-83-7

Elsa Barker—*War Letters from the Living Dead Man*
ISBN 978-1-907355-85-1

Elsa Barker—*Last Letters from the Living Dead Man*
ISBN 978-1-907355-87-5

Richard Maurice Bucke—*Cosmic Consciousness*
ISBN 978-1-907355-10-3

Arthur Conan Doyle—*The Edge of the Unknown*
ISBN 978-1-907355-14-1

Arthur Conan Doyle—*The New Revelation*
ISBN 978-1-907355-12-7

Arthur Conan Doyle—*The Vital Message*
ISBN 978-1-907355-13-4

Arthur Conan Doyle with Simon Parke—*Conversations with Arthur Conan Doyle*
ISBN 978-1-907355-80-6

Meister Eckhart with Simon Parke—*Conversations with Meister Eckhart*
ISBN 978-1-907355-18-9

D. D. Home—*Incidents in my Life Part 1*
ISBN 978-1-907355-15-8

Mme. Dunglas Home; edited, with an Introduction, by Sir Arthur Conan Doyle—*D. D. Home: His Life and Mission*
ISBN 978-1-907355-16-5

Edward C. Randall—*Frontiers of the Afterlife*
ISBN 978-1-907355-30-1

Rebecca Ruter Springer—*Intra Muros: My Dream of Heaven*
ISBN 978-1-907355-11-0

Leo Tolstoy, edited by Simon Parke—*Forbidden Words*
ISBN 978-1-907355-00-4

Leo Tolstoy—*A Confession*
ISBN 978-1-907355-24-0

Leo Tolstoy—*The Gospel in Brief*
ISBN 978-1-907355-22-6

Leo Tolstoy—*The Kingdom of God is Within You*
ISBN 978-1-907355-27-1

Leo Tolstoy—*My Religion: What I Believe*
ISBN 978-1-907355-23-3

Leo Tolstoy—*On Life*
ISBN 978-1-907355-91-2

Leo Tolstoy—*Twenty-three Tales*
ISBN 978-1-907355-29-5

Leo Tolstoy—*What is Religion and other writings*
ISBN 978-1-907355-28-8

Leo Tolstoy—*Work While Ye Have the Light*
ISBN 978-1-907355-26-4

Leo Tolstoy—*The Death of Ivan Ilyich*
ISBN 978-1-907661-10-5

Leo Tolstoy—*Resurrection*
ISBN 978-1-907661-09-9

Leo Tolstoy with Simon Parke—*Conversations with Tolstoy*
ISBN 978-1-907355-25-7

Howard Williams with an Introduction by Leo Tolstoy—*The Ethics of Diet: An Anthology of Vegetarian Thought*
ISBN 978-1-907355-21-9

Vincent Van Gogh with Simon Parke—*Conversations with Van Gogh*
ISBN 978-1-907355-95-0

Wolfgang Amadeus Mozart with Simon Parke—*Conversations with Mozart*
ISBN 978-1-907661-38-9

Jesus of Nazareth with Simon Parke—
Conversations with Jesus of Nazareth
ISBN 978-1-907661-41-9

Thomas à Kempis with Simon
Parke—*The Imitation of Christ*
ISBN 978-1-907661-58-7

Julian of Norwich with Simon
Parke—*Revelations of Divine Love*
ISBN 978-1-907661-88-4

Allan Kardec—*The Spirits Book*
ISBN 978-1-907355-98-1

Allan Kardec—*The Book on Mediums*
ISBN 978-1-907661-75-4

Emanuel Swedenborg—*Heaven and Hell*
ISBN 978-1-907661-55-6

P.D. Ouspensky—*Tertium Organum:
The Third Canon of Thought*
ISBN 978-1-907661-47-1

Dwight Goddard—*A Buddhist Bible*
ISBN 978-1-907661-44-0

Michael Tymn—*The Afterlife Revealed*
ISBN 978-1-970661-90-7

Michael Tymn—*Transcending the
Titanic: Beyond Death's Door*
ISBN 978-1-908733-02-3

Guy L. Playfair—*If This Be Magic*
ISBN 978-1-907661-84-6

Guy L. Playfair—*The Flying Cow*
ISBN 978-1-907661-94-5

Guy L. Playfair —*This House is Haunted*
ISBN 978-1-907661-78-5

Carl Wickland, M.D.—
Thirty Years Among the Dead
ISBN 978-1-907661-72-3

John E. Mack—*Passport to the Cosmos*
ISBN 978-1-907661-81-5

Peter & Elizabeth Fenwick—
The Truth in the Light
ISBN 978-1-908733-08-5

Erlendur Haraldsson—
Modern Miracles
ISBN 978-1-908733-25-2

Erlendur Haraldsson—
At the Hour of Death
ISBN 978-1-908733-27-6

Erlendur Haraldsson—
The Departed Among the Living
ISBN 978-1-908733-29-0

Brian Inglis—*Science and Parascience*
ISBN 978-1-908733-18-4

Brian Inglis—*Natural and Supernatural:
A History of the Paranormal*
ISBN 978-1-908733-20-7

Ernest Holmes—*The Science of Mind*
ISBN 978-1-908733-10-8

Victor & Wendy Zammit —*A Lawyer
Presents the Evidence For the Afterlife*
ISBN 978-1-908733-22-1

Casper S. Yost—*Patience
Worth: A Psychic Mystery*
ISBN 978-1-908733-06-1

William Usborne Moore—
Glimpses of the Next State
ISBN 978-1-907661-01-3

William Usborne Moore—
The Voices
ISBN 978-1-908733-04-7

John W. White—
The Highest State of Consciousness
ISBN 978-1-908733-31-3

Stafford Betty—
The Imprisoned Splendor
ISBN 978-1-907661-98-3

Paul Pearsall, Ph.D. —
Super Joy
ISBN 978-1-908733-16-0

All titles available as eBooks, and selected titles available in Hardback and Audiobook formats from www.whitecrowbooks.com

www.ingramcontent.com/pod-product-compliance
Lightning Source LLC
Chambersburg PA
CBHW031257110426
42743CB00040B/717